CIVIL PROCEDURE: PRECLUSION IN CIVIL ACTIONS

by

DAVID L. SHAPIRO
William Nelson Cromwell Professor of Law
Harvard University

TURNING POINT SERIES®

New York, New York
FOUNDATION PRESS
2001

Foundation Press, a division of West Group, has created this publication to provide you with accurate and authoritative information concerning the subject matter covered. However, this publication was not necessarily prepared by persons licensed to practice law in a particular jurisdiction. Foundation Press is not engaged in rendering legal or other professional advice, and this publication is not a substitute for the advice of an attorney. If you require legal or other expert advice, you should seek the services of a competent attorney or other professional.

Turning Point Series is a registered trademark
used herein under license.

 TEXT IS PRINTED ON 10% POST
CONSUMER RECYCLED PAPER

TURNING POINT SERIES

- **CIVIL PROCEDURE: TERRITORIAL JURISDICTION AND VENUE**
  Kevin M. Clermont, Cornell University

- **CIVIL PROCEDURE: CLASS ACTIONS**
  Linda S. Mullenix, University of Texas (Available March 2002)

- **CIVIL PROCEDURE: PRECLUSION**
  David L. Shapiro, Harvard University

- **CIVIL PROCEDURE: JURY**
  Nancy S. Marder, Chicago-Kent College of Law (Available November 2001)

- **CIVIL PROCEDURE: THE ECONOMICS OF CIVIL PROCEDURE**
  Robert Bone, Boston University, School of Law (Available August 2002)

- **CRIMINAL LAW: THE MODEL PENAL CODE**
  Markus D. Dubber, State University of New York at Buffalo (Available May 2002)

- **CONSTITUTIONAL LAW: EQUAL PROTECTION**
  Louis Michael Seidman, Georgetown (Available August 2002)

- **CONSTITUTIONAL LAW: RELIGION CLAUSE**
  Daniel O. Conkle, Georgetown (Available December 2001)

- **LEGISLATION: STATUTORY INTERPRETATION, 20 QUESTIONS**
  Kent Greenawalt, Columbia University

- **PROPERTY: TAKINGS**
  David Dana and Thomas Merrill, Northwestern (Available August 2001)

- **SECURITIES LAW: INSIDER TRADING**
  Stephen M. Bainbridge, UCLA

- **TORT LAW: PROXIMATE CAUSE**
  Joseph A. Page, Georgetown (Available November 2001)

*

For Ava

*

About the Author

David Shapiro is William Nelson Cromwell Professor of Law at Harvard University. After attending Harvard College and Harvard Law School, he served as an associate attorney in a Washington, D.C. law firm for five years and then as a clerk for Justice John M. Harlan during the 1962 Term of the U.S. Supreme Court. In 1963, he returned to Harvard as an Assistant Professor and was promoted to Professor in 1966. Except for visits at other law schools, and a term as Deputy Solicitor General in the U.S. Department of Justice from 1988-91, he has been teaching at Harvard ever since.

Professor Shapiro's scholarship has included a number of articles on aspects of American federalism and the American judicial system; his books include FEDERALISM: A DIALOGUE (1995) and co-authorship of the Second, Third, and Fourth Editions of HART & WECHSLER'S THE FEDERAL COURTS AND THE FEDERAL SYSTEM. In addition, he has participated in several American Law Institute projects; of special interest here is his work as Reporter and Adviser to the RESTATEMENT (SECOND) OF JUDGMENTS (1982).

*

Table of Contents

ABOUT THE AUTHOR VII

Preface 1
Chapter I. Introduction 5
  A. Scope 5
  B. Terminology 9
  C. The Rationale of The Doctrine of Preclusion ... 11
  D. The Structure of This Essay 18

Chapter II. Preclusion in a Subsequent Action Between the Same Parties in the Same Jurisdiction 22
Introduction 22
  A. Prerequisites of Recognition: Validity and Finality 23
  B. Claim Preclusion 32
  C. Issue Preclusion 46
  D. Cases in Which the First Proceeding Was Not a Coercive Civil Action Brought in a Court Exercising Personal Jurisdiction Over the Defendant. 60
  E. The Definition of a "Party" 68
  F. Procedural Issues 71

Chapter III. Application of the Rules of Preclusion to Those Not Parties to the Prior Action 74
Introduction 74
  A. Persons and Entities Treated "As If" They Were Parties 75

B. Other Non–parties 97

Chapter IV. Interjurisdictional Preclu-sion 119

Introduction 119

A. When F–1 Is a Tribunal of One State and F–2 Is a Tribunal of a Sister State 121

B. When F–1 Is a State Tribunal and F–2 Is a Federal Tribunal 135

C. When F–1 Is a Federal Tribunal 144

D. When F–1 Is a Tribunal of a Foreign Country and F–2 Is a Federal or State Tribunal in the United States 153

TABLE OF CASES 167

INDEX 171

CIVIL PROCEDURE: PRECLUSION IN CIVIL ACTIONS

*

PRECLUSION IN CIVIL ACTIONS

Preface

My fascination with the subject of judgments, and particularly with problems of preclusion, developed slowly over the years and resulted from a serendipitous (and probably symbiotic) combination of opportunity and interest. The opportunity knocked in the late 1960s, when my mentor (and idol) Benjamin Kaplan asked if I would like to join him as a Reporter for a revisiting of the *Restatement of Judgments*. The project, which eventually became the *Restatement (Second) of Judgments* (1982), proved both challenging and rewarding; all those who were involved in it are delighted that–while many of its propositions have not gone unchallenged–the *Restatement (Second)* has had a considerable impact on the development of the law and has contributed to the growing unification of an important and complex subject.

After Ben Kaplan and I completed a feasibility study for the ALI Council, we worked together on many of the core provisions on claim and issue preclusion that now appear in Volume I of the *Restatement (Second)*. Ben then had to resign because of his appointment to the Massachusetts Supreme Judicial Court, and after Geoffrey Hazard took his place as a Reporter, I too had to withdraw because of illness. Geoff went on to complete the project as sole Reporter, but fortunately, I recovered in time to rejoin the project as an Adviser for the last several years (including a sybaritic final Advisory Committee meeting in Bermuda).

During this work, I realized that the subject was fascinating for several reasons. First, it was one of the last outposts of common law essentially unaffected by statutes (though there were enough special statutes and procedural rules to give the subject a hybrid character that no aspect of the law can wholly escape), and thus the potential role both of the ALI and of commentators contributing to the field was greater than in areas more heavily codified. Second, this common law flavor gave the field a quality that is especially intriguing for an academic: it drew its principles from a combination of tradition, logic, and policy that didn't always mesh and that therefore made the field one of continuing movement and debate. Indeed, contrary to what one might expect, the topic was far from "static"; instead there was considerable controversy both over the proper scope and application of existing principles and over the development of new frontiers. And the controversy continues.

This realization led me to work and write in the field while the *Restatement* was in process and after the project was completed.[1] These writings have

---

1. For an even earlier piece, see David L. Shapiro & Daniel R. Coquillette, *The Fetish of Jury Trial in Civil Cases: A Comment on* Rachal v. Hill, 85 HARV. L. REV. 442 (1971).

ranged from a study of the issue preclusive effects of guilty pleas in subsequent civil proceedings,[2] to an exploration of the impact of federal judgments in subsequent state proceedings,[3] to a broader exploration of the role of preclusion in the federal system in Chapter 12 of the Hart & Wechsler casebook-coursebook-treatise on federal jurisdiction.[4] And at this writing, I have the special pleasure of serving on an Advisory Committee on another ALI project–one that is considering possible federal legislation relating to the recognition and enforcement of foreign country judgments.[5]

Thus, this effort to review the field of preclusion in all its aspects, to explore the principal current debates and frontiers, and to make the area more accessible to students and practitioners is a natural outgrowth of several decades of absorption with a topic that, to my continuing amazement, some find dry and unrewarding. If I succeed in convincing the reader that this impression is mistaken, and that the field is not only important but provocative and stimulating as well, I will be more than content.

My thanks for making this project possible, more readable, and less vulnerable, go to a number of

2. David L. Shapiro, *Should a Guilty Plea Have Preclusive Effect?,* 70 Iowa. L. Rev. 27 (1984).

3. David L. Shapiro, *State Courts and Federal Declaratory Judgments,* 74 Nw. U. L. Rev. 759 (1979).

4. Richard H. Fallon, Jr., Daniel J. Meltzer & David L .Shapiro, Hart & Wechsler's The Federal Courts and the Federal System ch. 12 (4th ed. 1996).

5. *See* American Law Institute International Jurisdiction and Judgments Project, Report (2000).

people and organizations, especially to Professors Daniel Meltzer and Larry Kramer, for their extraordinarily helpful comments on the manuscript, to Kelly Jaske for her research assistance, to Jim Coates and Maura Kelley for their editorial and production assistance, and to Foundation Press (a division of Westgroup), for its continuing and unstinting support.

Chapter I

Introduction

A. Scope

The subject of judgments and their legal and practical consequences is one of enormous breadth, and no work of modest scope can hope to cover it all. Thus the first task is the important one of describing the principal focus here, to indicate those aspects that are sufficiently on the margin to deserve attention—even though not in depth—and to delineate the topics that fall entirely outside the reach of this undertaking.

Those who labor in the judgments vineyard, and especially those who worry about the interjurisdictional consequences of a judgment, often distinguish between questions of "recognition" and questions of "enforcement." The terms are used to distinguish between the consequences of a judgment in a subsequent action ("recognition") and the availability of, and techniques for, effectuation of the relief specified in the judgment ("enforcement")—usually the payment of money or an order to act or to refrain from acting, but sometimes the declaration of a status or right, or the determination of an interest in property.[1] The principal focus here–as in the *Restatement of Judgments*—is on the first of these: the content and scope of the "recognition" of a judgment in a subsequent action. Of course, questions of recognition and of enforcement are not always easily separated, in part because a judgment not entitled to recognition is clearly not entitled to enforcement.[2] But such questions of enforcement as the techniques of obtaining money owed by a judgment debtor in the forum that entered the original judgment or in another forum, or of securing compliance with a decree (or punishing its violation) in the same or a different forum, do fall outside the scope of this book.

Another subject related to this project, but not within its core, is that of the grounds and procedures for obtaining relief from a judgment—matters covered in the federal courts primarily by Federal Rule of Civil Procedure 60(b). Once again, the issues of "recognition" and the ability to obtain relief are not always separable: for example, in an action in which the defendant asserts the defense of "bar" (on the basis of a prior judgment in his favor on the

1. As stated in the RESTATEMENT (SECOND) OF CONFLICT OF LAWS, Introductory Note preceding § 93 (1971), in discussing the effects of the judgments of other jurisdictions: "A foreign judgment is recognized ... when it is given the same effect that it has in the state where it was rendered with respect to the parties, the subject matter of the action and the issues involved. A foreign judgment is enforced when, in addition to being recognized, a party is given the affirmative relief to which the judgment entitles him."

2. *See* RESTATEMENT (THIRD) OF THE FOREIGN RELATIONS LAW OF THE UNITED STATES § 481 cmt. b (1987).

same claim), the plaintiff may be able to resist the defense on the same ground that would permit relief from the judgment under Rule 60(b). But in most instances, that overlap does not exist: until and unless relief is obtained from the judgment by the prescribed means, the judgment is entitled to recognition in the ways and to the extent discussed here.[3]

Still another important boundary line of this essay rests on the distinction between civil and criminal proceedings. The effect of a criminal proceeding in a subsequent criminal proceeding is largely governed by state and federal constitutional prohibitions against double jeopardy, and that topic is worthy of full-scale treatment in itself.[4] Moreover, notions of finality that are widely accepted in civil proceedings give way in the criminal context to the availability of post-conviction relief, through the writ of habeas corpus or other, less common writs, especially when the problem involves the legality of continuing incarceration.

But the impact of a criminal adjudication in a subsequent civil proceeding is at least closely relat-

3. For comprehensive treatment of the topic of relief from a judgment, see RESTATEMENT (SECOND) OF JUDGMENTS ch. 5 (1982).

Because the *Restatement (Second)* will be frequently referred to in this and the remaining chapters, it will be cited hereafter simply as RSJ. And in order to cut down on the frequency of footnotes, citations to RSJ will often be incorporated in the text (as will *infra* and *supra* references to text discussions).

4. For an excellent survey and analysis of the topic of double jeopardy, see CHARLES H. WHITEBREAD AND CHRISTOPHER SLOBOGIN, CRIMINAL PROCEDURE ch. 30 (4th ed. 2000).

ed to the core of this study, and is treated here, as is the impact of certain quasi-judicial determinations—especially those by administrative and arbitral tribunals. Moreover, the contrasts and similarities between preclusion in civil and in criminal cases (in the same or a different jurisdiction) are sufficiently striking and informative to deserve mention, even if not full-scale treatment.[5]

Finally, a number of "doctrines" bear a kinship to the doctrines of preclusion but, once again, do not lie at the heart of the study and thus will be given at most passing mention. Foremost among these are (1) the concept of the "law of the case"— the notion that ordinarily a court should not reexamine a ruling that it has made at an earlier stage of the same litigation unless the prior ruling was explicitly made subject to later revisiting; (2) the rule of "prior action pending"–that when a second action in a second court closely parallels a prior action brought elsewhere, the second court should stay its hand until the first action has been completed, unless (of course) there is some strong reason not to; (3) the doctrine of "election of remedies"—a doctrine that is in many ways a precursor of the law of preclusion, and that is still sometimes confused with it, but that, properly confined, relates primarily to extra-judicial conduct that, under the governing substantive law, may deprive a claimant of a particular form of relief (*see* RSJ § 25 cmt. m,

5. Comparisons will also be drawn, along the way, to the treatment of claim and issue preclusion under other systems for adjudicating civil controversies.

illus. 23–25); and (4) the doctrine of stare decisis, *i.e.,* the role of precedent in shaping the course of future judicial decisions.[6]

A backward glance over this scope note will confirm that most of it is devoted to a description of what is not covered—a bit like the technique of carving an elephant by chipping away everything that doesn't look like an elephant. But the remainder of this introduction—which is devoted to questions of terminology, to the rationale underlying preclusion doctrine, and to the structure of the chapters that follow—is designed to give the reader a fuller sense of the range of topics that do lie within the compass of this work.

B. Terminology

"Res judicata," said one wry observer of the field, "is hard enough."[7] And it is made even harder by the failure of courts and commentators to agree on the appropriate terminology—even on the proper use of the term "res judicata" itself. Thus, this note on terminology is placed at the beginning to establish a vocabulary for use in the remaining chapters.

6. The relationship of this doctrine to the rules of preclusion is perhaps most apparent when considering the proper boundaries of issue preclusion with respect to issues of law. *See infra* pp. 53–54.

7. Howard M. Erichson, *Interjurisdictional Preclusion*, 96 MICH. L. REV. 945, 945 (1998). The full sentence, in an article advocating a bright line approach to interjurisdictional preclusion (*see infra* ch. IV), is: "Res judicata is hard enough already."

But it is important to remember that the absence of a solid consensus means that you will find courts and other commentators using different terms from those used here, and that as a result, translation will sometimes be required.

The principal terms to be used here, and in my view the most useful and descriptive, are "claim preclusion" and "issue preclusion"[8]—terms originally coined (I think) by Professor Alan Vestal and now adopted by the *Restatement (Second)*, and by many commentators. The former term describes the situation in which a prior judgment precludes a second action on a claim, and the latter describes the situation in which a determination in a prior action precludes litigation of an issue in a later proceeding. A further useful refinement of "claim preclusion" is that the effect of a judgment for plaintiff is often said to "merge" the plaintiff's claim in that judgment, and the effect of a judgment for defendant is often said to "bar" a subsequent action on the claim that was disposed of in the prior action. A surprising amount of the subject matter of the recognition of judgments may be accommodated under these rubrics.

Some older terms, found in earlier decisions but no longer in common use, are "estoppel by verdict" and "estoppel by judgment" But the chameleon-like character of "res judicata" (literally, "the thing adjudicated") still haunts us. In the *Restatement (Second)*, and many other places, the phrase is used

8. And their corresponding adjective forms: "claim-preclusive" and "issue-preclusive."

as a blanket term to describe the entire field of the recognition of judgments, but it is also commonly used as a synonym for "claim preclusion," and the task for the reader is to figure out which usage applies. If the phrase is used here—and I hope it will be infrequently—it will be used in the *Restatement* sense, unless it appears in a quote.

The descriptive term "issue preclusion" happily takes the place of a more mysterious duo that is, sadly, still alive and kicking: collateral and direct estoppel. "Collateral estoppel," the more common of the two, describes the preclusive effect that determination of an issue will have in precluding relitigation of that issue in a subsequent action on a different claim. "Direct estoppel"—its lesser-known relative—describes the preclusive effect of the determination of an issue in those rare instances when a second action is allowed on the *same* claim as that asserted in a prior proceeding. Fortunately, the less cryptic term "issue preclusion" handily covers both situations.

C. The Rationale of The Doctrine of Preclusion

The doctrine of preclusion has taken some fairly hard knocks. It is, according to one wise judge, "universally respected but actually not very well liked."[9] And the Supreme Court once said that it

9. Riordan v. Ferguson, 147 F.2d 983, 988 (2d Cir.1945) (Clark, J., dissenting).

renders "white that which is black, and straight that which is crooked."[10]

If these views have merit, why *is* the doctrine one that is both unpopular and respected? And will the recent trend to give the doctrine even broader application serve only to tilt the balance further towards hostility on the part of litigants, commentators, and courts?

One might open the discussion by asking why a judgment should have any consequences beyond that of any other opinion about the proper resolution of a controversy—one that the parties are free to accept if they wish but also to reject if either side wishes to contest the conclusions reached by bringing all or part of the controversy before some other tribunal for a second opinion. The idea might seem strange to one trained in the American legal tradition, but it is not all that foreign to our thinking. After all, even within American legal systems, some decisions are subject not simply to appellate review (which may be wholly discretionary) but to "de novo" review, entitling the parties to start again from scratch. And the idea of "advisory" (*i.e.,* nonbinding) decisions by juries or arbitration panels has become an important feature of the Alternative Dispute Resolution movement. Indeed, even if a second opinion could freely be sought, a person who has come out on the short end of an adjudication would in all probability accept that result, and not throw good money after bad, unless that person had

10. Jeter v. Hewitt, 63 U.S. (22 How.) 352, 364 (1859).

a bottomless pocket and found some irrational delight in the litigating process.

The notion that a person should not be forced to accept a result as binding is especially appealing when there appears to be some good reason for revisiting the matter—for example, a change in the controlling law, newly discovered information that was not reasonably available before, or some other basis for concluding that the result of relitigation (in whole or in part) might well be different.[11] Moreover, the constant tension in our procedural system between the desire to do justice to a litigant despite a procedural lapse and the desire to bind a litigant to his lawyer's decisions in the interests of orderly procedure may too often be resolved in favor of the latter. Should a client be limited to a hard-to-win malpractice action against his attorney if the attorney has carelessly failed to litigate adequately every aspect of the client's case? Or should the client be allowed, at least in some circumstances, to renew the claim, or part of it, and perhaps to compensate the adversary and the judicial system for any additional burden by paying some or all of the additional costs—win or lose?

Hard as these questions may be, the answer usually given is that there are powerful reasons weighing in favor of preclusion—reasons that, in general, trump the arguments for freely allowing relitigation. At its core, this argument rests on the role

11. *Cf.* Edward W. Cleary, *Res Judicata Reexamined*, 57 YALE L.J. 339 (1948) (advocating more liberal allowance of "claim splitting").

of a duly recognized judicial tribunal in the resolution of disputes. If a final, valid judgment served only as the tribunal's advice on how a controversy should be resolved, leaving it to other tribunals (or even other officials) to consider the controversy anew if they and the parties wished, it would be hard even to think of the initial tribunal as a "court" in the accepted sense. And indeed, the need to recognize the finality of judgments—their immunity from reopening or nullification at the hands of the executive or legislature (as well as the oft-repeated canon that the courts do not sit to render "advisory opinions") is fundamental to the status of the federal courts under Article III of the Constitution[12] and of the courts of many states.

But perhaps this argument about the nature of judicial tribunals, and the need for their judgments to be recognized as final and authoritative (subject only to the normal course of appeal and review) is more relevant to the notion of enforcement than to questions of recognition, and within the sphere of recognition, more relevant to claim preclusion than to issue preclusion. After all, if a money judgment

12. For cases elaborating and applying the requirement of finality as necessary to the function of a federal court under Article III of the Constitution, see, *e.g.*, Hayburn's Case, 2 U.S. (2 Dall.) 408 (1792); Chicago & So. Air Lines v. Waterman S.S. Corp., 333 U.S. 103 (1948); Plaut v. Spendthrift Farm, Inc., 514 U.S. 211 (1995). For a discussion of these cases and other decisions, and of the range of views about the proper scope of the judicial function in our federal and state courts, and in other legal systems, see RICHARD FALLON, JR., DANIEL J. MELTZER & DAVID L. SHAPIRO, HART & WECHSLER'S THE FEDERAL COURTS AND THE FEDERAL SYSTEM 102–07 (4th ed. 1996).

could not be collected, or if a judicial decree ordering or prohibiting action could not be given teeth through the power to punish for contempt, a court would really be little more than a formal version of an advice column in the newspapers. And the very concept of the role of duly-constituted tribunals as an alternative to self-help would be undermined if not undone.

Yet preclusion doctrine—particularly its application to "recognition" of a judgment—does not stop here. An argument about the essential nature of a judicial system might come close to spending itself if the law simply provided that a losing party was obligated to comply with a judgment, or to satisfy its demands, until and unless that judgment was superseded by a later, inconsistent judgment. Even if the rationale could plausibly extend to protection of the winner against any subsequent assault on the judgment itself by the loser in the first action (the core of the doctrine of "claim preclusion"), it is surely more of a stretch to extend the argument about the inherent nature of courts to some of the more esoteric reaches of claim preclusion doctrine. And it is even more of a stretch to use it to defend the doctrine that prevents relitigation of an *issue* either as between the same parties, or in a lawsuit between the loser and one not even involved in the prior litigation. Indeed, many judicial systems fully worthy of the name take a far narrower view than we do of the proper scope of claim preclusion and barely recognize the doctrine of issue preclusion at all.[13]

Thus justifications, if they do exist, must be found in less formal, more pragmatic grounds. And there are several. First, and perhaps foremost, is the concept of repose. The finality of a judgment in its fullest sense, allows the loser as well as the winner, to get on with his life; to put a controversy over a claim, or even a part of a claim or an issue embedded in the claim, behind him and to move on to other things and, if necessary, other contests. In this sense, the rationale supporting preclusion doctrine is not unrelated to one of the principal purposes of the statute of limitations. And unlike the existence of limitations periods, preclusion doctrine has the added force of an adjudication to support foreclosure of further contest.

A related justification lies in the often invoked argument that any system of justice must strive not only for truth and accuracy but also for the avoidance of excessive costs. For a winning party to have to relitigate a claim already decided in his favor imposes costs not only on him—both financial and psychological—but also on the public in the form of judicial expenses not paid for by the parties themselves. Indeed, for the loser to be entitled to reliti-

13. For brief summaries of the approaches to claim and issue preclusion (particularly issue preclusion) in other legal systems, see Robert C. Casad, *Issue Preclusion and Foreign Country Judgments: Whose Law?,* 70 Iowa L. Rev. 53, 61–70 (1984); Michael J. Waggoner, *Fifty Years of* Bernhard v. Bank of America *Is Enough: Collateral Estoppel Should Require Mutuality But Res Judicata Should Not,* 12 The Review of Litigation 391, 394 n. 9, 402 n. 34 (1993).

gate a matter already determined even against one who has not litigated the matter before may well impose costs on the system itself that it ought not to bear (and that would be difficult to quantify and impose on the previous loser as a "tax" for relitigating). And another, less tangible cost to the system is the loss of "prestige" (for want of a better word) that attends the existence of inconsistent and even conflicting results. That may well be a cost worth bearing, as we often do in the furtherance of other interests. But the lack of assurance that a second adjudication will yield a "better" or more "accurate" result militates against a general authorization of relitigation solely on the assumption that a second consideration is more likely than the first to get things right. (Indeed, if this assumption were sound, would it follow that a third consideration is more likely to be correct than the second?)

Of course, full realization of this criterion might militate in favor of a "bright line" test that required preclusion regardless of the circumstances and that avoided the costs inevitably attending a more flexible approach to the preclusion issue itself. After all, how much do the parties and the system save if the question of preclusion is one so complex that it becomes time consuming and expensive to determine whether relitigation is indeed precluded, and if that determination is often made in favor of allowing relitigation to ensue? In the absence of a bright-line, predictable standard, preclusion doctrine might actually end up *increasing* the costs of litigation.

Yet try as we may to achieve simplicity and the fullest measure of predictability, there are too many possibilities for injustice in the application of absolute preclusion rules, and too many areas of continuing controversy, to give full effect to a bright line test. For example, the loser in the first litigation may have been deprived of an adequate opportunity to present his position—and the deprivation may even raise questions of constitutional dimension if the loss is to bar him from litigating again. And in other instances, interests that transcend those of the parties, and even of the judicial system, may demand the opportunity to relitigate as a matter of substantive policy. Thus, the story of preclusion doctrine is, perhaps inescapably, one of the struggle to achieve a balance between the competing claims of repose, predictability, and the avoidance of inconsistency on the one hand, and on the other, the demands of substantive policy and of the particular circumstances when those demands support the arguments for relitigation.

D.   The Structure of This Essay

The approach to the topic taken here parallels to some extent that adopted in the *Restatement (Second)*, but opts for some important differences in coverage and organization. In general, the effort is to begin with the most clear-cut instances of preclusion; then, building on that background, to explore some of the more debatable areas on the frontiers of preclusion doctrine; and finally to consider the added problems presented when the question of preclusion arises in a second action in a different jurisdiction.

Thus, Chapter II focuses on the application of preclusion doctrine in the context of a second action between the same parties in the same jurisdiction. Even in this area, where the arguments for preclusion are the strongest and most straightforward, difficult and controversial questions persist: When does a judgment attain the requisite degree of validity and finality to be entitled to claim preclusive or issue preclusive effect? How should a "claim" or "issue" be defined for preclusion purposes? What of cases in which the first proceeding was not a civil adjudication in a judicial tribunal but an administrative or arbitral proceeding, or a criminal prosecution? When should the arguments for preclusion be overridden by special circumstances warranting relitigation? And finally, what are the problems in determining whether a "party" to the second action was also a "party" to the first?

Chapter III, while holding constant the assumption that the first and second actions are brought in the same jurisdiction, turns to the application of preclusion to those not parties to the initial action. This topic in turns break down into several subtopics. First, when should persons and entities be treated as if they were parties to the prior action for purposes of imposing the burdens and bestowing the benefits of preclusion law? (This subject brings into play the significance of a range of legal relationships, and the consequences of formal or informal representation—including the burgeoning topic of the binding effect of a class action on the nonparticipating members of the class.) Second, with respect to those who are not to be treated as parties for the reasons just stated, when if ever, may they be saddled with the burdens, or enjoy the benefits, of the outcome of a prior adjudication? Both questions, and especially the former, bring us to the frontier of preclusion doctrine, and indeed, the question of burdening a non-party under these circumstances raises not only policy issues of the respect to be accorded interests in litigant autonomy, but also issues of due process—of the proper extent of one's right to a "day in court."

Finally, Chapter IV, building on all that has gone before, introduces the issue of "interjurisdictional" preclusion. First, the Chapter explores this issue in the context of the American federal system, looking initially to the situation in which the initial forum (F–1) is one state of the Union and the second forum (F–2) is another state. Then, the Chapter turns to the question of preclusion in the context of state-federal relations, asking first about the situation in which F–1 is a state court and F–2 a federal court, and then about the even more difficult problems presented in the converse case—where F–1 is a federal court and F–2 a state court.

The essay concludes by considering the play of preclusion doctrine in the international setting— specifically, the case in which F–1 is a tribunal in a foreign country and F–2 a state or federal tribunal in the United States. Here, we are concerned with such matters as the source of law governing preclusion, the significance of the quality of justice administered in F–1, the nationality of the parties, the role of "reciprocity" (of how F–1 treats American judgments), and the significance of international conventions and other treaties.

Thus, even with all the matters excluded from our scope—or only lightly touched on in passing—there is a lot to discuss. And my overall goal in this discussion is to provide for students and practitioners an accessible, conversational, somewhat opinionated, not too heavily footnoted treatment of the topic that is at the same time comprehensive, useful, and supported by sufficient authority that one who wishes to go more deeply into any facet of the field has the tools to begin.

CHAPTER II

PRECLUSION IN A SUBSEQUENT ACTION BETWEEN THE SAME PARTIES IN THE SAME JURISDICTION

Introduction

In teaching and writing about this subject over the years, I have learned the value of hypotheticals—especially simple ones—in talking about difficult, abstract concepts, and nowhere is this lesson more apt than in the area of preclusion. Thus, in setting the stage for this chapter—and to some extent the next two as well—let me posit a simple case of a three-car collision in which each of the three drivers (Alice (A), Bruce (B), and Carla (C)) suffers personal injury and each car incurs property damage. Assume further that each driver has a colorable claim of liability against each of the other drivers with respect to all the items of personal injury and property damage.

This simple hypothetical can, and will, be embellished in many ways to illustrate a range of problems. Other hypotheticals, as well as real cases, will enter into the discussion as it progresses. But I hope this basic case—which I will refer to as "The Accident"—will serve as a convenient vehicle (for want of a better word) to illustrate the basic concepts and their limitations.

A. Prerequisites of Recognition: Validity and Finality

Assume that after The Accident, A sues B in a state court, alleging negligence by B and seeking damages for her personal injuries. Under what circumstances will the determinations made in this suit be entitled to recognition (*i.e.*, to claim preclusive and/or issue preclusive effect) in a subsequent action between the same parties in the same state? What, in other words, are the essential conditions that must be met before preclusion doctrine comes into play?

The *Restatement (Second) of Judgments* (cited, for convenience, as RSJ) tells us, and the point is generally accepted, that before "recognition" may be accorded, there must be a valid, final judgment (RSJ §§ 1–14). And looking first to the prerequisite of validity, the *Restatement* tells us that the three components are adequate notice (RSJ §§ 2–3), territorial jurisdiction over the defendant (RSJ §§ 4–10),[1] and subject matter jurisdiction over the controversy (RSJ §§ 11–12).

---

1. "Territorial jurisdiction"—a term that does not appear in the *Restatement*—is here used to encompass the range of issues raised by the geographical limits on the authority of a court to render a binding judgment. These limits may apply to "personal" jurisdiction (RSJ § 5), jurisdiction over property (RSJ § 6), and jurisdiction over status (RSJ § 7).

1. *Notice and Territorial Jurisdiction.* For two principal reasons, the necessity of adequate notice and of territorial jurisdiction need not detain us long. First, the need to satisfy these requirements is universally accepted—indeed in many instances is a *constitutional* prerequisite for a binding judgment— even though their precise content is a matter of continuing evolution and debate. Second, the issues at the heart of that debate (when and to whom is notice required and when is it adequate? when has a person done enough to warrant the exercise of territorial jurisdiction over him, his property, his assertion of an interest in property, or his status— for example, as a parent, child, or spouse?)—lie at the margin of our concern.[2]

Several points are especially relevant to our topic, however.

First, as the Federal Rules of Civil Procedure— particularly Rule 12(g) and (h)—make clear, objections to notice or to territorial jurisdiction are easily waived; indeed, one must cut square corners to preserve them. Thus, simply appearing in the action may be sufficient to establish "validity" with respect to either or both of these prerequisites. And in some jurisdictions, even one who raises a valid and timely objection in the trial court may end up forfeiting that objection if, after the trial court has rejected it, he chooses to go ahead and litigate the

2. Problems of territorial jurisdiction deserve and, fortunately, have received a book of their own in this series. KEVIN M. CLERMONT, CIVIL PROCEDURE: TERRITORIAL JURISDICTION AND VENUE (1999).

merits. A party may therefore be able to challenge the validity of a judgment in a later action only if he has stayed out of the first action altogether—a risky alternative at best.

Second, even though the validity of a judgment is beyond challenge if the question of recognition arises in a later proceeding, it may be possible (by following appropriate procedures) to obtain relief from the judgment in the rendering forum. For example, suppose the plaintiff met the constitutional and statutory requirements for adequate notice, but the defendant did not receive *actual* notice before the entry of a default judgment. Under these circumstances, the defendant—relying on such procedural devices as Federal Rule of Civil Procedure 60(b)—may be able to obtain a vacation of the judgment if he can show due diligence, the existence of a colorable defense on the merits, and compliance with any other requirements imposed by the jurisdiction that entered the judgment.

2. *Subject Matter Jurisdiction*. The final requirement for a judgment to be valid—that the court have jurisdiction over the subject matter—is more complex and more controversial.[3] To begin, the definition of "jurisdiction over the subject matter" is an elusive one. It ranges from federal constitutional limitations on the powers of a federal court,

3. For a fuller, and somewhat more argumentative, treatment of the materials discussed here, see Karen Nelson Moore, *Collateral Attack on Subject Matter Jurisdiction: A Critique of the* Restatement (Second) of Judgments, 66 CORNELL L. REV. 534 (1981).

to explicit statutory provisions dividing subject matter authority among judicial tribunals at both the federal and state levels (and between federal and state courts), to questions that are sometimes described as "jurisdictional" but shade over into substantive issues of regulatory authority.[4] Despite this range of possible meanings, the traditional view was that a judgment by a court that lacked subject-matter jurisdiction was "void"—even if the court had considered and rejected a challenge to its subject matter jurisdiction in the course of the proceeding. Then, in several decisions, the Supreme Court held that, on the federal level, subject matter jurisdiction could not be re-examined (*i.e.*, collaterally attacked) if the question had been decided in favor of jurisdiction in the original action,[5] or (at least with respect to certain jurisdictional questions) if the question of subject matter jurisdiction *could* have been raised in the original proceeding but was not.[6] But in two later cases, the Court did permit collateral attack in a subsequent action—in one case on the basis of special interests embedded in the doctrine of sovereign immunity,[7] and in the

4. As an example of the last category, see Crowell v. Benson, 285 U.S. 22, 62 (1932) (describing the question of the existence of the employment relationship, for purposes of determining coverage by a federal workers' compensation law, as a question of "jurisdictional fact[].")

5. *See* Stoll v. Gottlieb, 305 U.S. 165 (1938).

6. *See* Chicot County Drainage Dist. v. Baxter State Bank, 308 U.S. 371 (1940). Both this case and Stoll v. Gottlieb, 305 U.S. 165 (1938), are discussed in Moore, *supra* note 3, at 539–41.

7. United States v. U.S. Fidelity & Guar. Co., 309 U.S. 506 (1940) (holding the prior decision of a bankruptcy referee "void,"

other on the basis of specific congressional legislation limiting the adjudication of certain matters to federal court.[8]

Against this shifting background, both the first and second *Restatement of Judgments* struggled with the question whether a judgment by a court lacking subject matter jurisdiction was "valid" for purposes of subsequent recognition. The response of the *Restatement (First)* (in § 10) was to limit collateral attack on this ground and then to list five rather vague and broadly stated factors that might support the allowance of such an attack—factors that, taken in sum, appeared to drive a stake close to the heart of the rule. The response of the *Restatement (Second)* was to move further in the direction of limiting collateral attack. Subject matter jurisdiction—narrowly defined—remains a prerequisite for a valid judgment, but collateral attack is limited to cases of default judgments and to contested cases where there was a "manifest abuse of

and thus subject to collateral attack, because the sovereign immunity of the debtor against whom a claim had been asserted in the prior action deprived the referee of subject matter jurisdiction). But the present significance of this decision is in doubt, as indicated by the holding in United States v. County of Cook, Illinois, 167 F.3d 381, 389–90 (7th Cir.1999), *cert. denied,* 528 U.S. 1019 (1999). In that case, a divided court of appeals distinguished *USF & G,* and held the United States precluded from raising a sovereign immunity defense as a result of the judgment in a prior action.

8. Kalb v. Feuerstein, 308 U.S. 433, 438–39 (1940) (characterizing as "void" and "a nullit[y]" a state court foreclosure judgment rendered during the pendency of a petition filed in federal bankruptcy court).

authority," where the first judgment "substantially infringe[s] the authority of another tribunal,"[9] or where the rendering court lacked the capacity to make an "informed determination" and principles of procedural fairness militate in favor of collateral attack (RSJ §§ 11, 12). Moreover, even a default judgment is entitled to recognition (whether or not the court had subject matter jurisdiction) if the party seeking to escape its consequences received notice of the proceeding and then "manifested an intention" to treat it as valid *and* if failure to give the judgment effect would impair another person's substantial reliance on that judgment (RSJ § 66).

Now that we have come so far—and indications are that courts are moving in the same direction as the *Restatement*–the question is whether it would make sense to go even further and to treat subject matter jurisdiction like other issues in a proceeding, whether judgment is entered by default or not, and whether the issue is contested or not. Were this approach taken, a judgment that was not subject to challenge on grounds of lack of adequate notice or lack of territorial jurisdiction would be entitled to recognition, at least in the absence of a clear need to protect such interests as the immunity of a sovereign entity or the authority of another forum whose exclusive jurisdiction over the controversy operated to preempt the jurisdiction of the initial tribunal.[10] After all, a party who has notice of a

9. These two instances appear to overlap. An example of both may be a case in which a traffic court undertakes to grant a divorce and award custody of a child.

10. *See* Moore, *supra* note 3, at 562–63.

proceeding, and over whom the court has territorial authority, would be hard pressed to complain that his interests were unfairly impaired when he had a fair opportunity to raise that issue in the proceeding itself. And the interest in preserving the allocation of authority among tribunals is significantly protected by a court's obligation to recognize *sua sponte* a potential lack of competence over the subject matter.[11]

3. *Finality*. In addition to the requirement of "validity," a judgment must be "final" to be entitled to recognition. At least in the abstract, the latter requirement makes eminent sense because a purely tentative or interlocutory determination would appear by definition to be too shaky to have the harsh consequences that recognition may entail. But as always, the devil is in the details, and the difficulties of determining what "finality" means in this context have been considerable. To return to The Accident (*supra* p. 22)—after what may have been too long an absence—may finality attach to a denial of B's motion for summary judgment, to a determination of B's liability made in a bifurcated trial before a second hearing on the measure of A's damages, or to a judgment for either A or B while

11. *See, e.g.,* Mansfield, C. & L.M. Ry. v. Swan, 111 U.S. 379 (1884); FED. R. CIV. P. 12(h)(3); *see generally* RICHARD H. FALLON, JR., DANIEL J. MELTZER & DAVID L. SHAPIRO, HART & WECHSLER'S THE FEDERAL COURTS AND THE FEDERAL SYSTEM 1580–83 (4th ed. 1996) (hereafter HART & WECHSLER); HART & WECHSLER 2000 Supp. 224–25.

an appeal from that judgment is pending?[12]

In general, an interlocutory order of any kind—be it a preliminary injunction, a denial of a dispositive motion (like a motion to dismiss or for summary judgment), or a partial judgment (on one of several issues)—is not considered final for preclusion purposes in view of its preliminary character. And this general rule is well-adhered to in the context of claim preclusion. But if a particular issue has been resolved in a manner that seems to settle that issue for purposes of the litigation—at least as far as the rendering court is concerned—there is authority (including RSJ § 13) for regarding the determination as final for purposes of issue preclusion in another action.[13] The soundness of this distinction is debatable, since the question of when an issue has been sufficiently resolved in an ongoing litigation is not always an easy one, and since an across-the-board, brighter line might be more valuable to

12. Comparison with the rules of double jeopardy in criminal cases is instructive. Normally, jeopardy "attaches" in a criminal proceeding—and operates to preclude a second prosecution for the same offense—when the jury is sworn in a jury trial case, or when the first witness is sworn in a bench trial. *See* CHARLES H. WHITEBREAD & CHRISTOPHER SLOBOGIN, CRIMINAL PROCEDURE 855–56 (4th ed. 2000). The rationale appears to be that the constitutional protection extends to the very process of being subjected to trial, and not merely to the burden of relitigating a claim or issue already resolved. (But there are, of course, significant exceptions to the double jeopardy rule, notably that a second prosecution may normally be brought if the first proceeding ended in a conviction that was reversed on appeal. *See id.* at 856–61.)

13. An important opinion, relied on in RSJ § 13 (*see* cmt. g Reporter's Note), is Lummus Co. v. Commonwealth Oil Ref. Co., 297 F.2d 80, 89 (2d Cir.1961), where Judge Friendly said: " 'Finality' in the context here relevant [issue preclusion] may mean little more than 'that the litigation of a particular issue has

litigants than one that is less distinct and more
context-sensitive.

A more important question—in that it is more
likely to arise and has more significant consequences when it does—is whether finality attaches
to an appealable decision before the opportunity to
appeal has expired or, if taken, before the appeal
has been resolved. The Restatement (RSJ § 13 cmt.
f), and many courts, say yes. The reasoning seems
to be that the alternative—given the slow pace of
the appellate process in most jurisdictions—is likely
to be an unacceptable delay before recognition of
the judgment is accorded. (And a further justification may lie in the fact that when appeals are
taken, the odds of reversal are certainly well below
50%.) But the cost, as some jurisdictions acknowl-
edge in insisting on exhaustion of available appeals
before finality attaches,[14] is that a judgment may
have been given recognition in another proceeding
even though that very judgment has subsequently
been reversed on appeal (thus giving rise to the
very inconsistency that the principle of preclusion
is, in part, designed to prevent). Two possible remedies—or at least palliatives—for this problem are
(1) for the court in which the later action is pending
to stay its hand, at least until the opportunity for
appeal has run, and perhaps longer if the appeal is
expedited, and (2) for a court that has accorded
recognition to a judgment that is later reversed to

reached such a stage that a court sees no really good reason for
permitting it to be litigated again."

14. The divergence among jurisdictions on this question is
reported in Howard M . Erichson, *Interjurisdictional Preclusion,*
96 MICH. L. REV. 945, 972–73 (1998).

grant relief from its judgment, particularly if special circumstances can be shown. Given the costs associated with the latter approach, including those that will be incurred if a second trial is required, the former seems markedly better.

B.   Claim Preclusion

1.   *The Rule.* The basic rule of claim preclusion, to quote Judge Henry Friendly in another context, is "beautifully simple, and ... simply beautiful."[15] A valid and final judgment is conclusive between the parties, except on appeal or other direct review, as follows: (1) a judgment for the plaintiff merges the plaintiff's claim in the judgment and normally gives him a new claim on the judgment; and (2) a judgment for the defendant operates to bar a second action on the same claim (RSJ § 17).[16] So stated, the rule is followed in every American jurisdiction, and in many foreign jurisdictions as well.

There is implicit in this rule an important policy judgment, and buried in it a number of difficult and controversial issues. Nevertheless, the basic outlines are clear and important. Thus, for example, in the case involving The Accident that was posited at the outset of this section—in which A has sued B

15. Henry J. Friendly, *In Praise of* Erie—*And of the New Federal Common Law,* 39 N.Y.U. L. Rev. 383, 422 (1964).

16. Omitted from this paraphrase is the third sub-paragraph of § 17, which deals with issue preclusion and is discussed below, in section C.

for her personal injuries—a valid and final judgment for A that includes an award of damages terminates A's ability to sue on the claim and creates in A a new claim on the judgment. The new claim can be enforced through the procedures provided in the jurisdiction and is entitled to full faith and credit in other domestic jurisdictions. And a judgment that B is not liable for the damages alleged operates to bar another action by A against B on the same claim.

The policy judgment underlying the rule has a double edge. On the one hand, although existing joinder practice in most jurisdictions (for example, Rule 18 of the Federal Rules of Civil Procedure) allows a plaintiff in A's position to join as many claims as she then has against the defendant in a single action, the rule of claim preclusion does not penalize a plaintiff for failing to do so; only the particular claim defined by reference to The Accident is merged in the judgment if A prevails, and barred from reassertion if A loses. The rationale for this limit on the scope of preclusion is the reasonable one that the efficiency gain from "coercing" A into combining unrelated claims in a single suit would be minimal at best. Indeed, there might well be a net loss if A felt compelled to join these unrelated claims in order to preserve them when in the normal course, A might choose to forgo them entirely. On the other hand, the rationale of the preclusion doctrine itself, as outlined in Chapter I, does support the imposition of the rules of merger and bar with respect to the very claim that was the subject of the initial action.

The problems buried in the interstices of the rule are several. To begin, it is often said that to have claim preclusive effect, a judgment must be "on the merits," but as we shall see, that term has become so misleading as to be less than worthless, and it seems more appropriate to list (as the *Restatement (Second)* does in RSJ § 20) those preliminary judgments that do *not* have claim preclusive effect. Second, the consequences of the rule depend heavily on the definition attached to the notion of a "claim" and to the identity of a "party"—both matters that are dealt with in subsequent sections of this chapter. Finally, the clarity and predictability of the rule are clouded both by tradition, which leads to some strange results in particular contexts, and by the need to take account of special circumstances.

2. *What Constitutes a "Claim"?* If so much turns on the definition of a "claim," it is not surprising that this question has become an area of debate and development. And both the controversy and the present trend are tied to the evolution of more general rules of pleading and practice, as well as an increased interest in the economics of litigation. At a time when a plaintiff's choices were governed by the forms of action and the separate jurisdiction of courts of law and equity—or their echoes after they had ceased to exist in theory—a "cause of action" (the prevalent, and still popular, term before the notion of a "claim" became dear to the hearts of proceduralists) was quite naturally

confined by those choices. Thus if a plaintiff could not combine theories of tort and contract, or a request for damages and injunctive relief, in the court of her choice, she could hardly be penalized for failing to do so. But once law and equity were merged, and the forms of action dwindled down to one, judges saw the wisdom of combining the carrot of free joinder of theories and requests for relief with a stick. Failure to take advantage of the opportunities would, and should, result in loss of the ability to sue on a theory or to seek a form of relief that, consistent with principles of *both* fairness and efficiency, should have been joined in a prior action. Indeed, such a failure seems explainable (assuming reasonable knowledge of the governing law) only as the kind of strategically motivated conduct that, if allowed, would impose unnecessary expense on the courts and on the adversary. A party may rest her case entirely on one of several available theories if she wishes, but if she does, that decision should normally be binding.

For these reasons, the "transactional" view of a claim entered the picture. By now, that view has been accepted in federal jurisprudence, in the majority of states, and in the *Restatement (Second)*. As stated in RSJ § 24(1), a "claim ... includes all rights of the plaintiff to remedies against the defendant with respect to all or any part of the transaction, or series of connected transactions, out of which the action arose."[17] [18]

17. Section 24 goes on, in subsection (2), to explain that what constitutes a transaction or series of connected transactions is

Not all jurisdictions, of course, have chosen to adopt this broad definition,[19] and some have adopted it only in part. (Indeed, this variation among jurisdictions, here and elsewhere, makes especially interesting the questions of interjurisdictional recognition dealt with in Chapter IV—questions that would be far less complex if the level of consensus on preclusion problems approached unanimity.) But for those jurisdictions that have taken the plunge, the case of The Accident may provide some useful illustrations of the transactional approach in action. If A's tort suit against B ended in defeat, the transactional view would prevent A from later suing B on a different theory of common law

"to be determined pragmatically," looking to such factors as relation "in time, space, origin, or motivation," and such other factors as the parties' expectations and business usage.

18. The contrast with the prevailing rule in the context of double jeopardy is striking, at least at the federal constitutional level. After a considerable amount of backing and filling, the Supreme Court now adheres to the rule of Blockburger v. United States, 284 U.S. 299 (1932) (reinstated in United States v. Dixon, 509 U.S. 688 (1993) (5–4 decision)). Under this rule, the same act or transaction constitutes two separate offenses that can be tried separately if it violates two distinct statutory provisions, "each [of which] requires proof of a fact which the other does not." *Id.* at 716, 719 (quoting *Blockburger*). (Thus a separate trial for the same offense, or for a lesser included offense, is precluded, but little else.)

19. California, for example, has not. *See, e.g.,* Sawyer v. First City Financial Corp., 177 Cal.Rptr. 398, 400 (Cal.Dist.Ct.App. 1981); GEOFFREY C. HAZARD, JR., COLIN C. TAIT & WILLIAM A. FLETCHER, PLEADING AND PROCEDURE 1304 (8th ed. 1999); Erichson, *supra* note 14, at 973–74 (noting, with discussion of cases, that "[s]ome state courts . . . have not adopted the broad definition of a claim urged by the Second Restatement").

liability, or on a theory based on a special statutory right. And whether or not A succeeded in obtaining a judgment for damages for her personal injuries, she would thereafter be precluded from bringing a separate action against B seeking recovery for personal injuries whose extent was not fully known at the time of the initial action,[20] or for the damage to her car in the same accident, and from seeking some sort of injunctive relief against B, even assuming that some particular aspect of the case warranted such relief. Surely, in the absence of very special circumstances, these consequences are warranted by A's failure to seek recovery in the initial action on the basis of reasonably anticipated but as yet not fully known injuries, of alternative theories, or of grounds for additional kinds of relief. And on the infrequent occasions when they are not, especially when the modification of a decree granting continuing relief seems justified by a change in circum-

20. For an excellent discussion of this rule, its hardships and limitations, see JOSEPH W. GLANNON, CIVIL PROCEDURE 438–39 (3d ed. 1997). As Glannon notes, the rule (as stated in RSJ § 25 cmt. c) would apply in the case of a plaintiff who sued and recovered for an eye injury and later discovered that an additional consequence of the injury was severe and frequent migraine headaches. But in some instances, as noted in text, relief from the rigor of the rule may be available if the applicable requirements for relief from the original judgment can be met. Also, as Glannon states, *id.* at 439 n. 4, "[The] so-called 'two-disease' rule, which allows an asbestos plaintiff to sue for later-developing cancer even if she was previously aware of a separate injury from exposure (such as asbestosis), is now clearly the majority approach.... [This exception may spread to cases in which] the later 'injury' is not a separate disease, but simply an unexpected consequence of the first."

stances, the appropriate remedy is, and should be, to obtain some form of direct relief through Rule 60(b) or its equivalent (*see, e.g.*, RSJ §§ 13, 71).

The concept of a "transaction" is far from self-defining, and in some instances, it is affected by tradition, business practices, or the underlying substantive law. (The significance of substantive considerations, which crop up throughout the field of preclusion, poses a continual challenge to the notion of a "trans-substantive" law of preclusion—a challenge that, in my view, creates a productive tension between the forces of uniformity and diversity.) Again, to give some examples drawn from the *Restatement* and supported by case law, a claim on a running account includes all monies owing up to the time the action is brought. But if there is an undertaking to make a series of payments that are considered "separate"—as when represented by a series of bond coupons or promissory notes—the plaintiff may sue on any one or more of the obligations separately and seriatim (RSJ § 24 cmt. d). And in certain breach of contract cases, the plaintiff may choose to treat the contract as still in effect and sue only for damages for the specific default, or may treat the breach as a total repudiation and sue for damages for breach of the entire agreement (RSJ § 26 cmt. g). Finally, in certain tort cases, as in certain damages actions for nuisance, the plaintiff may choose to sue only for the harm to date, or may sue for all past and future harm (RSJ § 26 cmt. h).

In an action by A against B, is a counterclaim by B (a counterclaim for personal injuries in The Accident) part of the "claim" for purposes of the rule? No, it's not, but for many of the reasons supporting the rule of claim preclusion itself, a solid majority of American jurisdictions have adopted, by statute or procedural rule, a requirement that a counterclaim arising out of the same transaction or occurrence as the original claim must be asserted in the original proceeding or be forever barred (*see, e.g.*, Federal Rule of Civil Procedure 13(a)). And as the *Restatement*, supported by some case authority, recognizes, the reality of the claim preclusion rule itself requires that, whether or not a jurisdiction has such a compulsory counterclaim statute or rule, a counterclaim should not be allowed to be asserted in a subsequent action if its effect would be to nullify the first judgment (RSJ § 22(2)(b)). Thus if A sues B for damages for breach of contract, and obtains a valid judgment by default, B should not be allowed to undo the judgment by bringing a subsequent action for rescission and restitution on grounds of mutual mistake (RSJ § 22 cmt. f, illus. 9). Indeed, to permit such a subsequent action under these circumstances would, in effect, allow B belatedly to litigate the original claim by casting as a new cause of action what is in essence a defense to the original claim.

3. *The Broadening of the Rules of Bar: Herein of the Transformation of the Requirement of a Judgment "On the Merits"*. Although the term "on the merits" is still in use to describe the preclusive

effect of a judgment, the term has been abandoned in the *Restatement*, and more generally, because of its ability to mislead: to create the impression that *only* a judgment rendered after a full hearing on the issues can have claim preclusive effect. That is no longer true, if it ever was, and the extension of the claim preclusive effects of a judgment has been especially marked with respect to pre-trial dismissals based on some flaw in the plaintiff's presentation or prosecution of his case. Once again, not all jurisdictions agree on all the particulars, but there is a clear consensus that a full hearing on the issues is not required. Not only will a settlement of the dispute have claim preclusive effect (unless the parties agree otherwise); many other dispositions short of a hearing on the merits will also bar a subsequent action unless otherwise specified.

At one time, a dismissal on demurrer, even without permission to file an amended pleading, operated only as a determination of the precise ground on which the demurrer was based, but today the federal courts and many state courts have reversed the presumption; such a dismissal (even if for an inadvertent omission of some critical allegation) will bar a second action on the claim stated (or purported to be stated) unless leave to amend is given or it is otherwise provided that the dismissal is without prejudice. And the same consequences generally follow from dismissals based on failure to prosecute or on failure to comply with the procedural requirements of the rules of the forum. The remedy, in other words, is limited to direct review of the decision, or an appeal to the court entering the judgment to reconsider its decision. In a procedural system that, in general, is not characterized by traps for the unwary, and that gives reasonable opportunity for compliance with the rules and for relief from their severity, this broadening of the scope of claim preclusion seems both fair and efficient. Yet the occasions on which it may cause a client to suffer for a lawyer's carelessness do give some pause, and it is less than obvious that a remedy against the lawyer for malpractice is sufficient to eliminate the concern.

One case that continues to be puzzling under existing law in many jurisdictions is that of a dismissal based on the statute of limitations. Such a dismissal does generally operate as a bar to a second action in the same jurisdiction—and, in a jurisdiction that follows a transactional approach, should bar even a second action based on a different legal theory that affords a longer period in which to bring suit.[21] A more difficult problem arises, however, and is discussed below, in the context of the effect of such a dismissal on a later action in *another* jurisdiction whose statutory period has not yet run. *Infra* ch. IV, § A.

4. *Exceptions to the Rule of Bar.* Not every victory for the defendant operates to preclude a second action on the same claim (although, as we will see, dismissals that have no claim preclusive effect may

21. *See* 18 CHARLES ALAN WRIGHT, ARTHUR R MILLER & EDWARD H. COOPER, FEDERAL PRACTICE & PROCEDURE § 4441, at 367–68 (1981).

have issue preclusive consequences). A claim may be dismissed "without prejudice"—thereby explicitly giving the plaintiff the opportunity to file an amended complaint or to start another action on that claim. But even when no such expression is used in granting a dismissal, claim preclusion may not apply. Thus, the requirement of a judgment "on the merits" survives in the limited instances of certain "threshold" dismissals that, quite understandably, are viewed as permitting a second action satisfying the requirement whose existence led to the original dismissal. Foremost among these—and generally if not universally recognized as such—are dismissals based on lack of territorial or subject-matter jurisdiction, improper venue, or misjoinder or nonjoinder of parties (joinder as a party of a person or entity that should not have been joined, or failure to join as a party a person or entity that should have been joined) (RSJ § 20). More problematic, but still understandable, is a dismissal on the ground that the action has been brought prematurely—before it was "ripe" for prosecution.[22] And

22. RSJ § 20(2). An interesting case is Costello v. United States, 365 U.S. 265 (1961), in which the Supreme Court allowed a second action to be brought on the same claim after plaintiff's initial action had been dismissed for failure to file an affidavit that was a prerequisite to suit. The Court sought to justify its result, and to reconcile it with the provisions of FED. R. CIV. P. 41, by classifying the original dismissal as based on a lack of "jurisdiction." 365 U.S. at 285. Surely, calling the first dismissal jurisdictional—assuming that label was necessary to the result— was quite a stretch; failure to comply with a condition to suit is hard to consider "jurisdictional" in any of the accepted senses of the term. On the other hand, considerations of substantive law applicable to the particular requirement (of the filing of an

it is also generally recognized that a defendant's victory does *not* prevent a second action on the same claim—even in those jurisdictions that have adopted a "transactional" approach—when the first court lacked authority to grant relief on the theory now alleged, or of the type now sought (RSJ § 26 (1)(c)). This exception is a modern echo of the traditional limitations on claim preclusion resulting from the forms of action and the separation of law and equity. An argument against recognizing such an exception can be made if the second court is one in which all theories could have been presented, or all forms of relief could have been sought, had the initial action been filed there. But a willingness to allow the plaintiff leeway in the choice of the original forum cuts the other way and lends support to relaxation of the rigors of claim preclusion in this instance.

Finally, the *Restatement* recognizes, with some decisional support, the unusual case in which the nature of a statutory or constitutional scheme, or the existence of a public interest that transcends that of the parties, may warrant affording the plain-

affidavit) may lend independent support to the allowance of a second action.

(For further discussion of Rule 41, of the meaning of a dismissal "on the merits," and of the preclusive effects of a federal court judgment, see *infra* ch. IV, § C, and especially pp. 147–51.)

One commentary on the *Costello* case states that it "can be confined within reasonable boundaries if it is limited to dismissals that cannot be corrected through the liberal procedures available for the correction of error.... " LARRY L. TEPLY & RALPH U. WHITTEN, CIVIL PROCEDURE 818 (2d ed. 2000).

tiff a second bite at the apple (RSJ § 26(1)(d),(f)). Thus, while a change in the law since rendition of the final judgment is normally an insufficient reason for overcoming the interests in finality and repose that support the rule of claim preclusion,[23] a change in the law at the highest judicial level affecting a large class—as in a matter involving fair administration of a regulatory scheme or uniform, nationwide observance of an authoritative constitutional decision—may well support a relaxation of the claim preclusion rule.[24]

5. *Exceptions to the Rule of Merger.* Just as a defendant's victory does not always constitute a bar, a judgment for the plaintiff does not always merge the underlying claim in that judgment. Several examples may be drawn from the list in the

---

23. For a particularly difficult case involving the application of this rule, see Federated Dep't Stores, Inc. v. Moitie, 452 U.S. 394 (1981). In *Moitie*, although a judgment against several plaintiffs was reversed on appeal, one of the plaintiffs, who had chosen not to participate in the appeal, was held barred by the adverse trial court judgment from pursuing a subsequent action.

24. *See* RSJ § 26 cmt. e, illus.4 (based on White v. Adler, 43 N.E.2d 798 (N.Y.1942)), and illus. 6 (suggested by Griffin v. State Bd. of Educ., 296 F.Supp. 1178 (E.D.Va.1969)).

Illustration 6 to RSJ § 26 is especially interesting. It posits a case in which a class of black pupils and their parents sue unsuccessfully to invalidate a law on the grounds that it fosters school segregation, and decide not to appeal because the appeal is not warranted under existing law. But in a later decision, the Supreme Court holds unconstitutional a similar law of another state. Illustration 6 states that a second action on the same claim by the original plaintiffs is not barred because "the policy of nationwide adherence to the authoritative constitutional interpretation overcomes the policies [supporting preclusion.]"

preceding section. Thus a statutory scheme may
contemplate that after a landlord has successfully
brought an "emergency" action for eviction of a
tenant, he may bring a subsequent, "regular" action for rent owing up to the time of the eviction
(RSJ § 26 cmt. e, illus. 5). And as already noted,
supra p. 38, the substantive law may give the plaintiff an option to treat a breach of contract as either
partial or total, or to treat a nuisance as temporary
or permanent. As a further example, the parties
themselves may have agreed to, or the court in
rendering a judgment may have authorized, splitting the claim into several separate actions.[25] Finally, because of a desire to avoid a pointless regres-
sion, a judgment on a judgment (often required in
order to make a judgment in one jurisdiction enforceable in another) is not regarded as merging the
claim (*i.e.*, the judgment debt on which the action
was brought) in the second judgment, and an action
on that claim is still available until the judgment
debt is satisfied (RSJ § 18 cmt. j).

* * *

In sum, the rules of claim preclusion are broad,
and—in line with the increased openness of procedural opportunities—have become broader in recent
decades. But merciless as the rules can be, room has
often been made for exceptions to accommodate a
range of special needs and circumstances.

25. RSJ § 26(1)(a),(b). At least one state, Michigan, reverses
the presumption and permits splitting *unless* the party asserting
preclusion objected to the omission in the original action. *See*
Erichson, *supra* note 14, at 979.

C. Issue Preclusion

1. *The Rule.* Whenever a second action between the same parties is permitted, whether on the same or a different claim, an issue may arise that was determined in the first proceeding. In such instances, the rules of issue preclusion may come into play and, in effect, require that the determination of the issue in the first proceeding be given binding effect in the second. The basic rule, though more complex in its formulation, is concisely set forth in the *Restatement (Second)* (RSJ § 27): "When an issue of fact or law is actually litigated and determined by a valid and final judgment, and the determination is essential to the judgment, the determination is conclusive in a subsequent action between the parties, whether on the same or a different claim."[26]

The considerations of policy underlying the doctrine of issue preclusion are not as strong as those on which claim preclusion is based, and indeed issue preclusion is not a rule as widely recognized in the

26. As so stated, the rule of issue preclusion encompasses both "collateral estoppel"—preclusive effect in a second action on a *different* claim—and its lesser known relative, "direct estoppel"—preclusive effect in a second action on the *same* claim. An example of the latter is presented if a federal court action is dismissed for lack of subject matter jurisdiction (for example, lack of diversity of citizenship). While not precluding a second action on the same claim in a state court, the determination of lack of diversity would be preclusive in a second action in a federal court asserting diversity of citizenship as a basis of jurisdiction.

courts of other nations.[27] Perhaps the most critical difference between the two types of preclusion is that a question of issue preclusion does not even arise unless the underlying claim is one that may be litigated between the parties. In other words, if the assertion of a *claim* is precluded, the litigation never gets off the ground; but as a rule, litigation will go forward whether a particular *issue* is open for determination or not, and as a consequence, the factors of finality and repose play a weaker role.

27. *See* Robert C. Casad, *Issue Preclusion and Foreign Country Judgments: Whose Law?* 70 IOWA L. REV. 53, 61–70 (1984); Michael J. Waggoner, *Fifty Years of* Bernhard v. Bank of America *Is Enough: Collateral Estoppel Should Require Mutuality But Res Judicata Should Not,* 12 REV. LITIG. 391, 402 n. 34 (1993). In addition, Erichson, *supra* note 14, at 971–72, observes that on the basis of its civil law tradition, Louisiana "simply did not recognize issue preclusion" until it adopted a new statute in 1991, and it is unclear how the doctrine will develop in that state.

However, the rules of issue preclusion have been recognized by our Supreme Court as an aspect of double jeopardy protection, and indeed, have been given a liberal application in that context. *See* Ashe v. Swenson, 397 U.S. 436 (1970); WHITEBREAD & SLOBO-GIN, *supra* note 12, at 877–80. Perhaps one reason for the breadth of application in the criminal context is the narrowness of claim preclusion in that same context. *See supra* note 18. On the other hand, the nature of the defendant's constitutional right to a jury trial in a criminal case surely militates against the use of issue preclusion by the *prosecution* to compel a finding of fact in a second criminal proceeding. At this writing, there is a split among the federal circuit courts on this question. *Compare, e.g.,* United States v. Pelullo, 14 F.3d 881, 896 (3d Cir.1994) (rejecting application of issue preclusion against a defendant in a second criminal proceeding), *with, e.g.,* Pena–Cabanillas v. United States, 394 F.2d 785, 787–88 (9th Cir.1968) (approving application of issue preclusion in similar circumstances).

Given this distinction, the requirements for the application of issue preclusion are generally recognized as more rigorous, and the exceptions (discussed in the following section) are broader and more subject to the exercise of judicial discretion. At the same time, the need for predictability is a factor of importance if the benefits that accrue from not having to relitigate an issue already decided are to exceed the costs of determining whether issue preclusion should apply. Those benefits, undoubtedly implicit in what has been said in previous discussion, relate to the saving in time and expense to the parties and to the court; to the value perceived in consistency of result; to the lack of assurance that a second determination will be more "accurate" than the first; and to the repose that attends the knowledge that an issue once decided is settled, at least as between the parties.

Thus the first precondition for the application of issue preclusion—that the issue have been "actually litigated and determined"—in the prior action, finds no precise parallel in the doctrine of claim preclusion, now that the disposition of the claim no longer needs to have been "on the merits." The function of issue preclusion, under this formulation, is not to prevent litigation of an issue because it *might* have been litigated before, but rather to prevent *relitigation* of an issue because it *was* litigated before.[28]

28. In my view, this reasoning is compelling, and the rule should be confined, as the *Restatement* provides, to the prevention of *re*litigation, especially in view of the expansion of the

To illustrate, return to the hypothetical of The Accident (*supra* p. 22) and assume that the jurisdiction is (a) one without a compulsory counterclaim rule and (b) one that regards contributory negligence by a plaintiff as a defense that must be pleaded and that, if proved, is a complete bar to recovery. Assume also that in A's action against B, B does not plead A's contributory negligence as a defense, and the case is litigated to judgment solely on the question of B's alleged negligence. B may bring a later action against A for his personal injuries incurred in the accident, and the issue of A's negligence will be open to litigation—even if it presents an issue identical to the defense that might have been raised in the first action.[29] [30] Support for

scope of claim preclusion that has occurred under federal law and in most states. Despite early precedents in some jurisdictions indicating that, in the event of a consent or default judgment, issue preclusion would apply to every issue that would have to be resolved to support a contested judgment, most if not all American jurisdictions now accept the *Restatement* view. *See, e.g.,* Arizona v. California, 120 S.Ct. 2304, 2318–19 (2000) (describing this view as "standard preclusion doctrine"); *see also* JACK H. FRIEDENTHAL, MARY KAY KANE & ARTHUR R. MILLER, CIVIL PROCEDURE 689 n. 5 (3d ed. 1999). There is a question, however, about the status of a *litigated* issue if a default judgment is subsequently entered or a settlement later agreed upon. *See id.* (When the case is settled, the availability of issue preclusion is also affected by the terms of any agreement between the parties.)

Finally, it is worthy of note that in the United Kingdom, issue preclusive effect is extended to "necessary steps to the decision," even in the case of default judgments. Casad, *supra* note 27, at 62 (quoting G. SPENCER BOWER & A. TURNER, THE DOCTRINE OF RES JUDICATA 152–53 (2d ed. 1969)).

29. Of course, some issues of contributory negligence—the failure to fasten a seat belt, for example—may not be identical to

this result, in addition to that already mentioned (that issue preclusion is designed to prevent *relitigation*) lies in the desirability of eliminating any incentive to a party to litigate an issue *solely* to avoid being foreclosed from litigating it in a future lawsuit that may never materialize when for reasons of economy or strategy, the party makes a reasonable decision not to raise the issue in the case at hand.

The second requirement for application of the rule, and one also generally recognized in the U.S., is that the determination be "essential to the judgment." Thus in the case of The Accident, assume that B did plead A's contributory negligence as a defense. If the court, sitting without a jury, first found that neither party was negligent and then, on the basis of those findings, rendered judgment for B, under this formulation of the rule, the finding of A's lack of negligence would not have issue preclusive effect in a subsequent action by B against A.[31] The reason underlying this result is not as clear-cut as in the requirement that the issue be "actually litigated," but it still has considerable force. First, there is at least a possibility that, since the finding

the issues raised when a party is accused of *causing* an accident through lack of care. In other fact settings—for example, where the question is whether A ran a red light—the issue may be the same. Thus a close look at the particular allegations, and their context, is often required to determine whether the issue in the second case is sufficiently related to the issue in the first to bring the rules of issue preclusion into play.

30. Issue preclusion is likely to apply, however, to the determination made in the first action with respect to B's negligence.

31. *See, e.g.,* Cambria v. Jeffery, 29 N.E.2d 555 (Mass.1940).

as to A was not determinative, the judge may have paid less attention to that finding than he otherwise would have—may have treated it, in a sense, as dictum. Second, the finding itself is unappealable by the party who lost on the issue since that party (B) was the winning party in the case. (At least the finding is unappealable in a jurisdiction that requires a showing that but for the finding, the party appealing might not have lost the case.) On the other hand, if the jurisdiction rejects the *Restatement* limitation on issue preclusion, B's ability to appeal the finding as to A's negligence might be grounded in the harm that could result to B in a future case. Rejection of the *Restatement* rule might therefore lead to the taking of appeals that would not otherwise be necessary, or even permissible. Thus for reasons discussed below, the unavailability of an appeal would in itself constitute an independent basis for denying a non-essential finding issue preclusive effect.

But what if a finding constitutes one of two or more alternative grounds in support of the judgment—if in The Accident case, for example, there is a judgment for B on the basis of findings that A was negligent and B was not? In that situation, should there be any issue preclusion in a later action by B against A arising out of the same event? A, as the losing party, is in a position to appeal the correctness of both findings, but it is clear that neither one was itself essential to the result. Denial of preclusive effect to either finding might thus decrease the likelihood of an appeal (and save time and expense) where the losing party was reasonably certain that at least one of the alternative grounds would be upheld on the appeal, but would surely increase costs if either issue were to arise in a later lawsuit. [32]

The arguments for and against issue preclusion are sufficiently in balance that a switch of positions on the question from the first *Restatement* (preclusion on both issues) to the second (preclusion on neither, as stated in RSJ § 27 cmt. i) turned out to be one of the most contentious in the floor debates on the entire *Restatement (Second)*, and the Reporters' proposal carried only by a closely divided vote.[33]

Whichever approach is taken, several points should be noted. First, if there is an appeal, the principal argument against preclusion is no longer relevant, and preclusive effect should be given to an appellate decision even if it is based on alternative grounds (RSJ § 27 cmt. o). Second, while there is certainly an argument for a case-by-case approach to the problem of alternative grounds, adoption of this approach would, in my view, be a powerful example of the game not being worth the candle. The problem is sufficiently narrow, and the compet-

32. For a fuller, and forceful, presentation of the arguments favoring preclusion in this situation, see Jo Desha Lucas, *The Direct and Collateral Estoppel Effects of Alternative Holdings,* 50 U. CHI. L. REV. 701 (1983).

33. The Reporters placed heavy reliance on the reasoning of Judge Friendly in his opinion for the court in *Halpern v. Schwartz,* 426 F.2d 102 (2d Cir.1970)—a decision that has to some extent been qualified by the Second Circuit itself in later cases. *See* RICHARD H. FIELD, BENJAMIN KAPLAN & KEVIN M. CLERMONT, CIVIL PROCEDURE 1162–64 (7th ed. 1997).

ing arguments sufficiently close in every case, that a predictable, bright-line test seems preferable to a more ad hoc approach designed to fine-tune the result in each instance.

The rule as set forth in the *Restatement* provides for preclusion on "an issue of fact or law." The explicit extension of the rule to issues of "law" represents a gradual development, from a time when the concept related only to issues of fact—and indeed was referred to as "estoppel by record"—to a time when courts attempted to distinguish between "pure" issues of law and more case-specific matters, to the present, when courts and commentators recognize the value of preclusion on any determination of law as well as on findings of fact.[34] After all, as one commentator noted, a determination of law, unlike a finding of fact, does not depend on any "external reality" but rather on direct judicial perception, and thus may be more worthy of preclusive effect in subsequent litigation between the parties.[35]

But when it comes to issues of law, why isn't the doctrine of stare decisis—the effect normally accorded to judicial precedent—an adequate safeguard against the imposition of an undue burden on the

34. The story is told in Geoffrey C. Hazard, Jr., *Preclusion as to Issues of Law: The Legal System's Interest,* 70 Iowa L. Rev. 81, 89–90 (1984). For early cases in this development, see United States v. Moser, 266 U.S. 236 (1924); Commissioner v. Sunnen, 333 U.S. 591 (1948). For later cases taking a broader view, see Montana v. United States, 440 U.S. 147 (1979); United States v. Stauffer Chem. Co., 464 U.S. 165 (1984).

35. *See* Hazard, *supra* note 34, at 88–89.

parties and the courts? And why should the law remain static as between two litigants in a prior case if it is subject to change in any other litigation? These are not easy questions. In some situations, there may be a value in obtaining a more secure settlement of a question of law than the doctrine of stare decisis can provide—consider, for example, a breach of contract case in which the court decides an important issue of the nature of "consideration," followed by a second suit for a subsequent breach of the same contract. But the questions do at least suggest the need for caution in determining the range of situations in which relitigation of an issue of law will be barred. And indeed, as discussed in the next section, courts and commentators have recognized this need.

A final set of problems presented by the rule of issue preclusion is implicit in the statement of the rule: how is an "issue" to be defined? Here are some examples drawn from the *Restatement*, other sources, and my own (warped) imagination: Is a determination that A was "disabled" in year 1 the same (at least in the absence of proof of changed circumstances since the first judgment) as the question whether he was disabled in year 2? Year 20? In the case of The Accident, does a determination that A was not negligent in failing to stop at a stop sign (as B alleged in support of his defense of contributory negligence) preclude B from arguing (for the first time in a later suit against A) that A's negligence consisted of traveling at an excessive speed? What if, in the first case, a determination of B's negligence is based on a finding that B was legally intoxicated at the time of the accident, and the "ultimate" issue in a subsequent case is whether B was legally intoxicated at that time? And finally, what if the court in the first case determines the tax consequences of an arrangement under a specific contract, and an issue involving the same taxpayer and identical contractual provisions, but a different contract, arises in a subsequent case?

Once again, the approach to this problem has evolved over the years. In the era of the *Restatement (First)* and before, the tendency was to insist on complete identity,[36] and to distinguish between a finding of "ultimate" fact (*e.g.*, that B was negligent) and a finding of "mediate" fact (*e.g.*, that B was drunk). More recently, and as reflected in the *Restatement (Second)*, the tendency has been to expand the possibility of issue preclusion in several directions. Thus, the standard has become a more pragmatic one—one that looks to such factors as the relationship between the two claims, the reasonableness of requiring a party to produce all available evidence in support of a particular contention, the foreseeability at the time of the first litigation that the issue would arise in subsequent litigation, the likelihood that the passage of time or other circumstances would make a difference, and the importance attached to the particular question in

36. For example, a determination of the tax consequences of a contract would not result in issue preclusion on the question of the tax consequences of a different contract involving the same taxpayer, even if the relevant contract provisions were the same. *See* Commissioner v. Sunnen, 333 U.S. 591, 599–600 (1948).

the initial action (*see* RSJ § 27 cmt. c). Thus in the examples in the preceding paragraph, the argument for issue preclusion is persuasive in every case, except perhaps the one involving a 20-year gap between two lawsuits on the question of a disability. And even there, a court would be likely to take into consideration the nature of the disability.

As in other instances, the problem involves a choice between a clear, hard-edged test and a more flexible standard. Here, the choice has been to make the test a more flexible one, and in doing so, to move towards greater availability of issue preclusion. The choice is never easy, but this one may well be justified by the unnecessary rigor of the earlier approach, and perhaps also by the gap between the appearance of certainty and the reality of uncertainty that inhered in that approach.[37]

2. *Exceptions to the Rule.* A number of exceptions have been recognized—in the *Restatement* and in many jurisdictions—to the applicability of issue preclusion to a finding in a prior action.[38] In gener-

37. In particular, the Reporter's Note to RSJ § 27 cmt. j, emphasized the "inherent vagueness" and "difficulty of application" of the distinction drawn in many cases between findings of "ultimate" fact, which were given issue preclusive effect, and subsidiary findings of "mediate" facts, which were not. The Reporters concluded, and the *Restatement* commentary reflects the conclusion, that a better and more workable standard would be that described in the text: the importance attached to the question in the initial action and the foreseeability of its potential preclusive effect in later actions.

38. In this instance, it seems appropriate to quote in full the relevant black letter as a basis for the discussion in text. Follow-

al, these exceptions are warranted by the presence of one or the other (or sometimes both) of two considerations. First, some aspect of the initial proceeding may serve substantially to weaken its qualifications for preclusive effect in a subsequent action. And second, there may be an overriding public interest in allowing the issue to be relitigated in the subsequent action.

ing, then, is the list of exceptions to the rule of issue preclusion as set forth in RSJ § 28:

(1) The party against whom preclusion is sought could not, as a matter of law, have obtained review of the judgment in the initial action; or

(2) The issue is one of law and (a) the two actions involve claims that are substantially unrelated, or (b) a new determination is warranted in order to take account of an intervening change in the applicable legal context or otherwise to avoid inequitable administration of the laws; or

(3) A new determination of the issues is warranted by differences in the quality or extensiveness of the procedures followed in the two courts or by factors relating to the allocation of jurisdiction between them; or

(4) The party against whom preclusion is sought had a significantly heavier burden of persuasion with respect to the issue in the initial action than in the subsequent action; the burden has shifted to his adversary; or the adversary has a significantly heavier burden than he had in the first action; or

(5) There is a clear and convincing need for a new determination of the issue (a) because of the potential adverse impact of the determination on the public interest or the interests of persons not themselves parties in the initial action, (b) because it was not sufficiently foreseeable at the time of the initial action that the issue would arise in the context of a subsequent action, or (c) because the party sought to be precluded, as a result of the conduct of his adversary or other special circum-

The first of these considerations is the primary one, and is exemplified by several exceptions. Most broadly, a determination of an issue will not be given preclusive effect when—because of such factors as the relatively small amount involved, or the quality or extensiveness of the procedures available in the first action—the party to be precluded did not have an adequate opportunity or incentive to litigate the issue fully and fairly. (As additional examples, preclusive effect may be denied if the issue is one on which the party to be bound could not have appealed or otherwise obtained review, or if it was sufficiently unforeseeable at the time of the first action that the issue would arise in the context of the later suit.[39]) Also significant is the burden of proof in the two actions: issue preclusion is inappropriate if the party to be bound has a significantly lighter burden of proof in the second action than he did in the first.

Two further exceptions appear to fall more squarely under the second consideration—that of the public interest in allowing relitigation. One is the case in which the allocation of subject matter jurisdiction among courts supports the conclusion that the determination of an issue by the first court,

stances, did not have an adequate opportunity or incentive to obtain a full and fair adjudication in the initial action.

39. An example given in the *Restatement* (RSJ § 28 cmt. i) involves the determination in an initial action between the taxing authorities and the taxpayer that a property transfer has not occurred—a determination that then becomes relevant to a wholly different question of tax liability under a statutory amendment passed after the first judgment.

even though it had authority to make that determination in the particular context, should not operate to bind the second court when the issue is presented in a different (and usually more direct) context.[40] The other involves preclusion on an issue of law in a situation in which the question arises either in a wholly unrelated context or—even more clearly— after an intervening change in the generally applicable rule of law. In the former instance, denial of preclusion seems warranted by the value of allowing the court to consider the question of a possible change, restrained only by principles of stare decisis, when the controversies in the two lawsuits are so unrelated that the parties are in essentially the same position as two adversaries who have not litigated before. And in the latter, there is a clear interest in having everyone subject to the same rule of substantive law, especially when the effect of recognizing a different rule would be to cause competitive, or even less tangible, injury to persons subject to the less favorable rule. As an example, it would surely be inappropriate to allow one importer, on the basis of an earlier decision, to continue to

40. One example that might arise in a single jurisdiction: a court of general jurisdiction determines in a tort action that plaintiff and defendant are legally married, and the same issue then arises in a divorce proceeding brought in a court (of the same state) having exclusive jurisdiction over the marital relationship. Another, interjurisdictional example: a state court determines, in a contract action, that the defendant should prevail because the patent involved in the contract suit is invalid; the issue of validity then arises in a patent infringement action brought in a federal court having exclusive jurisdiction over such actions.

import goods duty-free when, as a result of a later decision by a higher court, other importers were required to pay duty on the same product.[41]

D. Cases in Which the First Proceeding Was Not a Coercive Civil Action Brought in a Court Exercising Personal Jurisdiction Over the Defendant.

This section deals with an assortment of instances in which some special feature of the initial proceeding may warrant either a denial of (claim or issue) preclusion or a more searching consideration of the question whether preclusive effect should be given. One set of cases arises when the first proceeding was a judicial one but was either not a civil action, or was not based on the exercise of personal jurisdiction over the defendant, or was one in which the claimant sought not coercive relief but only a declaration of rights. A second set involves those instances in which the first proceeding was prosecuted in a non-judicial forum—most commonly a proceeding in an administrative or arbitral tribunal.

1. *Judicial Proceedings.* In some civil proceedings brought in a judicial forum, territorial jurisdiction is based not on personal jurisdiction over the defendant but on jurisdiction over property. In many of these cases, the purpose of the jurisdiction is to determine respective interests in property, and

----

41. *See* United States v. Stone & Downer Co., 274 U.S. 225, 236–37 (1927).

in such cases, the effect of the "claim preclusive" effect of the judgment is limited by the nature of the jurisdiction and the purpose of the action. In other words, the judgment settles the interests of the parties in the property, but does not impose a personal liability on the defendant and does not have the same "transactional" claim preclusive effect that the same jurisdiction might accord in an action based on personal jurisdiction over the defendant. But if the requisites for issue preclusion discussed in the previous section are met, then there is no reason to deny that effect in a subsequent proceeding (RSJ § 30).

At one time, prevailing law in most jurisdictions allowed territorial jurisdiction over a person's property to serve as the basis for adjudicating a wholly unrelated claim against that person, but (unless the party, in appearing, gave express or implied consent) a judgment for the plaintiff would have claim preclusive effect only up to the value of the property in question. Today, as a result of the decision in *Shaffer v. Heitner*,[42] the ability to exercise territorial jurisdiction on this basis is, at best, a mere shadow of what it once was. Yet to the extent it still exists, the claim preclusive (but not the issue preclusive) effect is limited by the nature of the proceeding. Thus, a judgment for plaintiff on the claim will not preclude him from pursuing the same claim

42. 433 U.S. 186 (1977). For an excellent summary of the *Shaffer* decision, its effect, and the rare situations in which this basis for territorial jurisdiction still appears to exist, see KEVIN M. CLERMONT, *supra* note 2, at 65–67.

in a second action in which territorial jurisdiction is based on some other property or on jurisdiction over the person, but of course, any amount received as a result of the prior judgment will be credited against any subsequent judgment (RSJ § 32).

Two other kinds of civil actions prosecuted in a judicial forum that are accorded special treatment are (a) those involving adjudications of status, and (b) those seeking only a declaration of rights and/or obligations and not coercive relief. In the first of these—involving determinations of status—the typical cases fall into the area of family law, and involve such issues as separation, divorce, and custody. In these cases, it remains true that the authority of a court does not necessarily depend on territorial jurisdiction over the defendant[43] and thus the full measure of claim preclusion does not apply. For example, in a divorce proceeding in which the forum's authority to dissolve the marriage arises solely from the separate domicile of the plaintiff spouse in the forum state, the state would not have authority (without the consent of the absent spouse) to award alimony or child support against the absent spouse, and a separate proceeding to obtain such relief would therefore not be precluded (RSJ § 31).

In the second category—involving actions for declarations of rights and obligations—the forum's authority to render judgment may be founded on

43. For a summary of the various bases of territorial jurisdiction to dissolve a marriage, see RESTATEMENT (SECOND) OF CONFLICT OF LAWS §§ 70–72 (1971). For a summary of the bases of territorial jurisdiction to entertain other marital suits and suits involving custody, see *id.* §§ 75–77, 79.

personal jurisdiction over the defendant, but the purpose of the action, and of the statutes authorizing it, is to allow a plaintiff to obtain the determination without seeking coercive relief (in the form of an injunction or damages), and often in situations where coercive relief is unavailable.[44] While a judgment in a declaratory action should (indeed, must) be given issue preclusive effect if the requisites for according that effect are met, the very purpose of allowing such an action would be undermined if, for example, claim preclusion were taken to prevent a successful plaintiff from seeking other and further relief in a later action based on the assertion that the defendant had acted in a manner inconsistent with the declaratory judgment.[45] Moreover, issues not litigated in the declaratory action—perhaps because they were not foreseeable or because the plaintiff was seeking only a limited clarification of his rights and duties—should not be foreclosed in a later coercive action arising out of the same controversy. The ability to prosecute such an action and to raise issues not previously litigated, notwithstand-

44. Thus the Federal Declaratory Judgment Act, in 28 U.S.C. § 2201, states that declaratory relief may be granted in an appropriate case "whether or not further relief is or could be sought." For an example of a declaratory judgment action in which coercive relief (an injunction or damages) would have been unavailable at the time of the action, see American Mach. & Metals, Inc. v. De Bothezat Impeller Co., 166 F.2d 535 (2d Cir.1948).

45. The Federal Declaratory Judgment Act, in 28 U.S.C. § 2202, provides that after issuance of a declaratory judgment, "[f]urther necessary or proper relief ... may be granted" in order to effectuate the rights and duties determined in the declaratory action.

ing the general rules of claim preclusion, is therefore recognized in the *Restatement (Second)* (RSJ § 33).[46]

A final instance in which the nature of the initial judicial proceeding requires special consideration is one in which the first action consists of a criminal prosecution. Normally, the second action in this situation involves a different plaintiff from the public prosecuting authority in the first, and thus the question should perhaps be saved for Chapter III. But the problem can arise between the same parties—for example, when a criminal prosecution for theft of government property is followed by a civil action by the same government to recover the value of the property—and so may properly be considered here. And indeed, focusing on a subsequent action between the same parties helps to demonstrate why and how the rules of preclusion have been reasonably extended to these cases.

At one time, the rules of preclusion were held not to apply when the first action was criminal and the second civil. But the logic of the matter led courts and commentators to rethink the question. If, for example, a defendant is convicted of arson, with all the safeguards attendant upon a criminal trial, should that same defendant be allowed to relitigate the issue of his responsibility in a subsequent civil action for damages if—as is normally the case—the

46. For an endorsement of the approach of § 33, an enumeration of those jurisdictions that appear to have followed that approach, and a plea for similar endorsement in other jurisdictions where the law is unclear, see Comment, 48 UCLA L. Rev. 159 (2000).

elements of criminal responsibility are more than sufficient to establish civil liability and if the burden of proof that the plaintiff must bear is lighter in the second proceeding? Given the reasonableness of a negative answer to this question—at least if the criminal defendant was not disadvantaged by some particular procedural rule (like the reduced opportunity for discovery in a criminal case)—the availability of issue preclusion in this context has been widely recognized (*see* RSJ § 85).[47]

An acquittal in a criminal proceeding is a different matter. Although it may be based on a determination of law that, under the normal rules of issue preclusion, *would* be binding in a subsequent proceeding (if the determination was one that the government could have appealed), there are two reasons why a determination of fact in the defendant's favor should not furnish him with the sword or shield of preclusion in a subsequent action. First, appeals by the prosecution from adverse determinations of fact are normally not available, and second, the burden of proof that the prosecution failed to satisfy in the criminal action is significantly lighter than the burden on virtually any issue of fact in a civil action. Thus two of the exceptions to the availability of issue preclusion (*see* RSJ § 28(1), (4)) are relevant in most instances of acquittal.[48]

47. The question of claim preclusion, of course, would not arise, since the civil action could not have been joined with the earlier criminal proceeding.

48. But if an issue of fact arises in a context where the burden of proof in the prior criminal proceeding was the same as in the later civil proceeding, and an appeal was available to the

A final question in this area has proved to be a contentious one: whether the entry of a plea of guilty, or of nolo contendere, should have any issue preclusive effect in a subsequent civil proceeding. Following the rule of the *Restatement (Second)*— that to have preclusive effect, an issue must have been "actually litigated"—and the reasoning behind that rule, the proper answer would seem to be no, and the *Restatement* so provides (*see* RSJ § 85 cmt. b).[49] But not all jurisdictions agree, and a willingness to apply issue preclusion may stem from the facts that (a) as a matter of procedure (that at least to some extent is constitutionally required), a court may not accept a guilty plea without being satisfied that the plea is warranted, and (b) the consequences of a plea of guilty can be so drastic that it is unlikely to be entered casually. But guilty pleas do often result from bargains designed to save the risk averse defendant from the hazards of far more costly litigation and more draconian penalties. And a fear of issue preclusion in later litigation may itself operate to deter the very bargaining that is regarded as socially useful and desirable. Thus the *Restatement* rule seems the better choice.

Those jurisdictions permitting a guilty plea to have issue preclusive effect may well deny such effect to a "nolo" plea, thus giving prosecutors an additional bargaining chip. And those jurisdictions

prosecution (as in the case of the grant of a pretrial motion to suppress evidence), issue preclusion may well be appropriate.

49. *See also* David L. Shapiro, *Should a Guilty Plea Have Preclusive Effect?*, 70 Iowa L. Rev. 27 (1984); Haring v. Prosise, 462 U.S. 306, 316 (1983).

denying preclusive effect to a guilty plea may well allow the plea into evidence as an admission, to which the trier of fact may give weight in reaching a decision.

2. *Non-judicial proceedings*. The two types of "quasi-judicial" proceedings that may most commonly give rise to an assertion of preclusion in a later civil action are (a) proceedings before an administrative agency, and (b) proceedings before an arbitral tribunal. In each instance, the availability of preclusion has been recognized,[50] but at the same time, the need for a more searching inquiry has also been acknowledged (*see* RSJ §§ 83, 84). Among the factors worthy of a closer look are: the nature and purpose of the proceeding, the quality of the procedures adopted by the initial tribunal; the scope of and limitations on the tribunal's subject-matter jurisdiction; the existence and extent of available judicial review; and the possibility that according preclusive effect to a particular non-judicial determination may be inconsistent with a statutory scheme of remedies or some other legislative policy.[51]

50. For a list of relevant decisions as of the early 1980s, see RSJ § 83, Reporter's Note (administrative proceedings); *id.* § 84, Reporter's Note (arbitration proceedings).

51. Here, as elsewhere, claim and issue preclusion should be distinguished. As the *Restatement* notes (in the commentary to § 83), a non-judicial proceeding may not be entitled to claim preclusive effect if the proceeding itself (a rate-making proceeding, for example) did not involve adjudication of a legal claim, yet the determinations made may have issue preclusive effect with respect to issues litigated under procedural rules sufficiently

Thus, with respect to the quality of procedures followed, a court should determine whether the tribunal has adopted what the *Restatement* calls "the essential elements of [fair] adjudication," including the rights to present and rebut evidence, to formulate issues, to argue orally or in writing, and to have the tribunal apply the governing rules (of the contract or of the general law) to the facts as found. With respect to possible conflict with a statutory scheme of remedies, one instructive decision is *University of Tennessee v. Elliott,*[52] where the Court was willing to recognize the preclusive effect of an administrative proceeding with respect to a claim based on one statute (28 U.S.C. § 1983), but not another (Title VII of the Civil Rights Act of 1964), because the latter contemplated a right to de novo judicial consideration after the completion of the administrative process.

Finally, especially with respect to arbitration, a court should ordinarily honor any agreement between the parties with respect to the permissible preclusive effects of any determination.

E.   The Definition of a "Party"

As is so often true in this field, the core of the rule is almost self-evident; it is at the margins that

similar to those used in judicial proceedings. Conversely, the adjudication of a claim of legal right in a non-judicial forum may have claim preclusive effect but the proceeding may have lacked the elements of procedural fairness required for the application of issue preclusion under the standards described in the text.

52.   478 U.S. 788 (1986).

things get interesting and difficult enough to be of concern to courts and observers. So here, the question of how to define a "party" for purposes of the rules of preclusion considered in this and the following chapters begins with the near-platitude that a person or entity named in the pleadings is normally—indeed, almost always—included within the definition (RSJ § 34).

But once that proposition is established as a starting point, a number of questions necessarily arise. Are there situations in which some person or entity is named as a party but not regarded as one for preclusion purposes? And, conversely, are there situations in which a person or entity *not* named is nevertheless a party? (This question closely overlaps with a range of questions considered in the next chapter—*i.e.*, when will a non-party be treated as a party for preclusion purposes?—and indeed the distinction is primarily an organizational one rather than one having significant substantive consequences.) And finally, in what situations, if any, will preclusion be unavailable as between two parties to a prior litigation because they were not adversaries with respect to the claim or issue involved in that action?

On the initial question—in what situations will a named party in action No. 1 not be subject to preclusion in action No. 2—two instances are especially worthy of note.[53] First, the named party may

53. *See also* RSJ § 35 (dealing with the extent to which the incapacity of a party may prevent application of the rules of

not be the real party in interest but only a nominal party—for example, the original owner of a claim that has been transferred—and that fact may be known to the adverse party (*see* RSJ § 37). Second, the named party may be a party acting in one capacity in the first action (*e.g.*, in his individual interest) and in another in the second (*e.g.*, as a trustee). Surely in such a case, it would be prejudicial to the interest of the beneficiary in the second case to give preclusive effect to the determination in the first.

On the next question—asking whether and when one not named in the action may be bound as a party—I have already noted the close relation of this question to that of determining when one not named is bound *as if* he were a party, and to some extent, the choice between these categories is an arbitrary one. But a real party in interest who actually appears and litigates—for example, a patentee who is not named as a party but who defends the validity of a patent in an action brought against his licensee—would appear to fall into the first of these groupings (with respect at least to the issue of patent validity).

Finally, two persons may be parties in a litigation, but not adversaries with respect to a particular claim or issue, and thus the rules of preclusion as stated here would not apply. To return briefly to The Accident, if A sues B *and* C for negligence, and neither B nor C asserts a non-compulsory cross-

preclusion); *infra* ch. III(A)(3)(b) (discussing special problems involving the absent members of a class in a class action).

claim against the other, then any determinations made in the case will not have preclusive effect as between them under the rules considered so far—at least if B and C did not become adversaries in fact in the course of the litigation (*see* RSJ § 38).[54] Of course, in such a case, if a question were determined adversely to, say, B, then C (under the analysis in the next chapter) may be able to obtain the advantages of issue preclusion in a later action between B and C. But if that is so, it is not because of C's presence in the first case but only because the jurisdiction has abandoned the traditional requirement of mutuality in this context.

F. Procedural Issues

A few special points about the procedural aspects of the rules of preclusion are worthy of note.

First, preclusion—claim preclusion or issue preclusion—is considered an affirmative defense (as indicated, for example, in Federal Rule of Civil Procedure 8(c)), and thus if not raised by the defendant in a timely fashion, may itself be denied consideration by the court. But since the rationale of preclusion doctrine draws in part on the efficiency gains to the judicial system, the matter has been held to be one that a court may recognize on its own motion if it wishes.[55]

54. See FLEMING JAMES, JR., GEOFFREY C. HAZARD, JR., & JOHN LEUBSDORF, CIVIL PROCEDURE § 11.7, at 588 (4th ed. 1992).

55. *See* 18 WRIGHT, MILLER & COOPER, *supra* note 21, § 4405, at 33–34. For an example of a refusal to entertain a defense of

Second, if the defense of preclusion is not raised in a subsequent action—or is raised and is erroneously rejected—the second judgment normally will be given preclusive effect to the extent that it is inconsistent with the first (*see* RSJ § 15).

Third, if a judgment is entered that would be entitled to preclusive effect but then the case becomes moot in the course of an appeal, so that the appeal cannot be pursued, some jurisdictions (including the federal[56]) provide that the judgment being appealed should itself be vacated, in order to avoid the possibility that the judgment will be given any preclusive effect. (Query: shouldn't the inability to prosecute an appeal, at least from a court of original jurisdiction, result in a denial of issue preclusive effect to that judgment in any event?) But at least in the federal courts, as well as a number of other jurisdictions, a settlement of the case on appeal, or any other voluntary action by a party that serves to moot the appeal, will not warrant either vacation of the judgment being appealed or (at least in the absence of a binding agreement between the parties) the denial of preclusive effect to that judgment as between them.[57] Moreover, in these jurisdictions, such an agreement will not prevent the judgment from having whatever stare decisis effect it would normally have, and may not prevent other

preclusion that had not been timely raised, see Arizona v. California, 120 S.Ct. 2304 (2000).

56. *See* United States v. Munsingwear, 340 U.S. 36 (1950).

57. *See* United States Bancorp. Mortgage Co. v. Bonner Mall Partnership, 513 U.S. 18 (1994); *see also* HAZARD, TAIT & FLETCHER, *supra* note 19, at 1334.

parties from gaining the benefits of preclusion in a later action if the jurisdiction allows such benefits to be claimed.

Finally, as noted before, some defenses to an assertion of preclusion—like the lack of territorial jurisdiction in the initial action—are available in the very case in which preclusive effect is sought. But others, if available at all, may be raised only in a motion or other proceeding for relief from the judgment brought in accordance with the rules of the jurisdiction in which the judgment was entered.

CHAPTER III

APPLICATION OF THE RULES OF PRECLUSION TO THOSE NOT PARTIES TO THE PRIOR ACTION

Introduction

This chapter, which builds on the basic rules of claim and issue preclusion developed in Chapter II, deals with a range of issues involving the effects of prior judgments on persons who were not parties to that judgment. In doing so, it covers the spectrum from those who for various reasons are treated in some or all respects as if they were parties to those who may be saddled with the burdens, or claim the benefits of a prior judgment even though they were not, and cannot be treated as, parties to that judgment.

Many of these issues are relatively new, and many that have been around for a quite a while remain highly contentious. Indeed, in some respects—especially such questions as the possibility of burdening a non-party with the preclusive effects of a judgment—we may be on the frontier of significant change. And any such change would cut deeply into some fundamental notions of the nature of litigation and the proper scope of litigant autonomy.

In an area as contentious as this, there is no way to avoid expressing my own views of where the best resolution lies (and I wouldn't if I could). But when those views still represent the position of a minority (perhaps of only one), I will make every effort to distinguish between them and those that, at the date of this writing, appear to have gained general acceptance.[1]

A. Persons and Entities Treated "As If" They Were Parties

1. *Two Special Cases: Control and Agreement.* To begin the summary catalogue of instances in which a person (or entity) is treated for all purposes as a party—*i.e.*, in which that person may properly be subject to all the burdens and benefits of the rules of preclusion—two situations have evoked little if any disagreement. The first is the case in which a person not named as a party has actually taken control of the prosecution or defense (RSJ § 39).[2] Although proof of this fact almost inevitably requires going outside the record, such proof should not ordinarily be difficult, and the rationale for the result is a strong one: a person who has controlled

1. There are a number of helpful sources on this topic. In addition to material in the leading treatises on Civil Procedure, I have found James R. Pielemeier, *Due Process Limitations on the Application of Collateral Estoppel Against Nonparties to Prior Litigation,* 63 B.U. L. Rev. 383 (1983), to be especially useful.

2. For a leading decision so holding, see Montana v. United States, 440 U.S. 147 (1979).

all aspects of a litigation has little basis for arguing that he is entitled to another opportunity to litigate the claim or the issue adjudicated in the prior action.

One consequence of this rule is, in many instances, to resolve the question of the extent to which a government may be bound as if it were a party by a judgment in an action against one of its officers or employees. Such actions are not uncommon: take, for example, habeas corpus proceedings against a prison warden, or damage or injunction actions brought against a government officer either because the doctrine of sovereign immunity precludes an action against the government itself or because the plaintiff has some special reason for seeking a remedy against the officer involved, or both. In many such cases, the government under whose authority the officer acted, or is threatening to act, will take over the defense of the action, and when it does, the government will be treated as if it were a party by virtue of that fact.

(The issue is less certain when the government does not control the litigation, since at least some decisions allowing individual actions for relief that could not be obtained directly from the government rest in part on the rationale that the government, as a non-litigant, will not be bound.[3] To some

3. *See, e.g.,* United States v. Lee, 106 U.S. 196, 220–21 (1882). For a modern echo of this rationale, see the discussion in the concurring and dissenting opinions in Idaho v. Coeur d'Alene Tribe, 521 U.S. 261, 290–91 (O'Connor, J, concurring), 305–08 (Souter, J., dissenting) (1997).

extent, the uncertainty surrounding the preclusive effect of judgments against government officials is alleviated by three factors: (a) the stare decisis effect of the decision when the case involves an important question of law resolved by an appellate court, (b) support for the view that since the government is the "real party in interest," it should be bound as a party by the consequences of the litigation,[4] and (c) the notion that a decree in an action for injunctive relief brought against a government officer "in an official capacity" binds the officer's successors.[5] But the problem remains buried in the unresolved tension between the concept of sovereign immunity and that of government under law.[6])

Second, there is little doubt that a person may agree contractually to be bound in some or all respects as if he were a party to a particular litigation. Thus, if separate actions involving the same transaction are brought by different plaintiffs against the same defendant, all the parties to all the

4. *See, e.g.,* Duncan v. United States, 667 F.2d 36, 38 (Ct.Cl. 1981).

5. Provided that the plaintiff can show that the successor has continued to engage in the conduct in question. *See, e.g.,* Spomer v. Littleton, 414 U.S. 514 (1974). *Cf.* FED. R. CIV. P.25(d) (automatic substitution of public officer's successor as a party when original action was brought against officer "in an official capacity").

6. For further discussion of this vexing problem, see RICHARD H. FALLON, DANIEL J. MELTZER & DAVID L. SHAPIRO, HART & WECHSLER'S THE FEDERAL COURTS AND THE FEDERAL SYSTEM 1024 (4th ed. 1996) (hereafter cited as HART & WECHSLER); HART & WECHSLER 2000 Supp. 81–82; David L. Shapiro, *State Courts and Federal Declaratory Judgments*, 74 NW. U. L. REV. 759, 764–65 (1979).

actions may agree that the question of the defendant's liability will be definitively determined, one way or the other, in a "test case." In many instances, this technique may be one of the most effective for resolving a multi-party dispute.

The existence and effect of an agreement can get fuzzy at the edges, however, and indeed may at some point fade into the category of legal relationships, discussed below.[7] Does a purchase of stock in a corporation, for example, constitute an implied agreement to be bound—to the extent of one's ownership interest in the corporation—by any judgment for or against the corporation? Perhaps in this and other cases, courts should be hesitant to rely on notions of "implied consent" and should look directly to the question whether the legal relationship itself warrants treating a person as if he were a party.

2. *Legal Relationship Between the Party and the Non-party.* In a considerable number of situations, courts have recognized that the substantive legal relationship between the party to the initial action and the non-party to that action warrants treating the non-party in some or all respects as if he were a party. Each of these relationships, on close examination, has some special characteristics that warrant special treatment and/or the recognition of some limitation on the appropriate scope of preclusion with respect to the non-party. Thus, they con-

7. For a perceptive discussion, see Pielemeier, *supra* note 1, at 402–15.

stitute departures from the generally "trans-substantive" nature of the rules of preclusion, and in an essay of this scope, it would be inappropriate and fatiguing (believe me!) to go into these relationships (and accompanying special features) in any detail. Instead, the relationships will simply be listed here—by identification of the non-party—with a reference to the relevant section(s) of the *Restatement* for those who wish to pursue one or more in any depth.[8]

- A successor in interest to property, the status and ownership of which has been determined in a prior action (RSJ §§ 43, 44).

- A successor under a survival statute following (a) a judgment for or against the victim in a personal injury action and (b) the death of the victim (RSJ § 45).

- One entitled to bring a wrongful death action after (a) a judgment for or against the victim in a personal injury action and (b) the death of the victim (RSJ § 46).

- One entitled to bring an action to recover for his or her own losses as a result of a personal injury to another—as in the case of an action by a spouse for loss of consortium (RSJ § 48).

- A person having a relationship with another such that one is vicariously responsible for the conduct of the other (RSJ § 51).

8. This list, while not exhaustive, is reasonably comprehensive. It should, however, be considered in conjunction with the closely related cases of representation considered in the next section.

- One having the relationship of bailee or bailor to another, with respect to certain property (RSJ § 52).

- One who is an obligee of a "joint" (as opposed to a separate) obligation (RSJ § 53).

- One who is a co-owner of property (RSJ § 54).

- One who is the assignor or assignee of property (RSJ § 55).

- One who is the promisee or intended beneficiary with respect to a contract (RSJ § 56).

- One who is the indemnitor (by contract or operation of law) of another.[9]

- One who is an officer, owner, or part owner of a corporation; or an officer, owner, part-owner, or member of an unincorporated association (RSJ §§ 59, 61).

- A partnership, or person who is a member of a partnership (RSJ § 60).

In addition, certain legal relationships may have the limited preclusive effect that the discharge of a

9. Rules governing this relationship are set forth in RSJ §§ 57, 58. The first of these sections deals with the generally accepted practice of (and the limitations on) allowing a defendant to "vouch in" his indemnitor, *i.e.*, to give the indemnitor adequate notice of the action and an opportunity to take over the defense. When properly done, the effect of this procedure will be to bind the indemnitor to the court's determination of the indemnitee's liability to the plaintiff—whether or not the indemnitor has accepted the offer to participate. (Questions have been raised about this practice, especially when there is doubt about the territorial jurisdiction of the forum over the indemnitor and the indemnity relationship arises not from contract but from operation of law.)

judgment against one (for example, a co-obligor) will, to the extent of the value received, discharge the liability of the other (*e.g.*, RSJ § 50).

3. *Persons Represented by a Party to a Prior Action: Existing Law.* The notion that you may suffer the burdens, and reap the benefits, of a prior action because you were represented by a party to that action, is one of long standing, but one that has been recognized only in limited settings. The first major category embraces those instances where either by private arrangement or through operation of law, there is a pre-existing legal relationship between the party to the initial proceeding and the non-party. The second category—a category with one principal member—involves the preclusive effect of a class action on those members of the class who did not participate (or did not fully participate) in that action.

(a) *Fiduciary Relationships.*[10] Perhaps the classic examples of persons bound by a prior action because they were represented in that action are (1) a beneficiary of a trust who is bound by an action brought by or against the trustee as representative of the interests in the trust, and (2) a beneficiary of an estate who is bound by an action for or against the executor or other fiduciary entitled by law to represent the estate (RSJ § 41(1)(a),(c)). These are both cases in which private arrangements (the appointment of a trustee or executor by the settlor or

10. The *Restatement (Second)* properly eschews the term "privity" as more conclusory than descriptive. Indeed, the term does not even appear in the Index.

testator) combine with the legal consequences of
that appointment to designate the appointee as the
legal representative of the persons holding a benefi-
cial interest in the property being administered by
the appointee. In a related instance, the representative in the initial action has been appointed by
agreement between that person and the person to
be bound in the later action (RSJ § 41(1)(b)). Indeed, this last instance is in some respects the most
compelling because the person to be bound has
himself designated his representative for purposes
of the initial litigation.

Also related are those cases in which the representative in the initial action has acquired his representative capacity solely by operation of law (including, in some instances, appointment by the
court). These cases include: a representative of an
estate appointed by the court (or by operation of
law) when the testator has not named an executor;
a guardian or "next friend" of a minor; and other
guardians ad litem appointed by the court to represent an incompetent or absentee. A similar case,
though perhaps somewhat more problematic in its
implications, is one in which "[a]n official or agency
[is] invested by law with authority to represent the
person's interests" (RSJ § 41(1)(d)).

In all these cases, the binding effect of the initial
action has its limitations. It extends only to those
matters in which the representative acted, and was
duly authorized to act, in a representative capacity.
It is conditioned on compliance with any requirements of notice to the person represented, and may

be defeated by a showing that the representative was subject to a conflict of interest in the initial action, or failed to fulfill his duties of care as a fiduciary (RSJ § 42).

(b) *Class Actions*. Although the concept of the class action—that a person or persons may litigate on behalf of a class as plaintiff or defendant—has a long and respected history in both the United Kingdom and the United States,[11] the concept has been marked by at least two significant developments. First, the notion that a class is appropriate for purposes of litigation has been separated from the notion of a class as a pre-existing group with a range of interests in common and ready access to the means of communication and selection of leaders.[12] Second, the class action device has not only expanded in the range of controversies to which it has applied (a development that parallels the burgeoning of cases in which a defendant's alleged malfeasance may affect a wide and diverse group), it has also come to be recognized both as a way of avoiding the need for joinder and as a means of reaching a resolution that will bind all members of the class.[13] The latter development, which is of principal concern here, has been neither smooth nor easily reconciled with fundamental notions of the

11. *See* STEPHEN C. YEAZELL, FROM MEDIEVAL GROUP LITIGATION TO THE MODERN CLASS ACTION (1987).

12. *See id.*

13. For an excellent, comprehensive discussion of the long and complex road to the general acceptance of this idea, and of the difficulties that continue to plague it, see Geoffrey C. Hazard,

role of individual autonomy in litigation. And at this writing, some of the most basic questions about the prerequisites of a judgment binding on the class remain subject to vigorous debate.

For present purposes, I assume that all members of the class are situated within the territorial jurisdiction of the forum in which the class action is brought and in which it goes to judgment (after trial or, more frequently, as a result of pre-trial disposition by motion or by settlement).[14] Also, I assume that (a) the court has made a timely decision that the action may proceed, in whole or in part, as a class action,[15] and (b) if the action has been concluded by settlement, the court has approved the settlement—including the amount to be paid to the lawyers (either in addition to or as part of the amount recovered by the plaintiff class) as fair. To focus on the principal issue of preclusion

Jr., John L. Gedid & Stephen Sowle, *An Historical Analysis of the Binding Effects of Class Action Suits,* 146 U. PA. L. REV. 1849 (1998). Two Supreme Court decisions of particular significance in this development are Supreme Tribe of Ben Hur v. Cauble, 255 U.S. 356 (1921); and Hansberry v. Lee, 311 U.S. 32 (1940).

14. In the important (but cryptic) decision in Phillips Petroleum Co. v. Shutts, 472 U.S. 797 (1985) (discussed *infra* at p. 90), many members of the plaintiff class were non-residents of the state in whose courts the class action had been brought.

Although historically, class actions against a defendant class were not infrequent, they are relatively uncommon today, and the discussion here will focus on questions of preclusion as they affect members of a plaintiff class.

15. *I.e.,* that the court has found, at least provisionally, that the customary preconditions to certification (*see, e.g.,* FED. R. CIV. P. 23) have been met.

arising in modern class action litigation, may members of the class who did not participate fully in the action be *bound* by the result as a matter of the law of preclusion, and if so, to what extent? (The question of the extent to which such persons may *benefit* from the disposition, either as a matter of claim or issue preclusion, is discussed in Section B(2) of this Chapter.) For example, if a class member who did not take timely advantage of an opportunity to "opt out" of the class is dissatisfied with the result—either because the class was defeated or because its "victory" (through settlement or otherwise) is seen as inadequate by that class member—may he pursue his claim independently against the defendant?

The very idea that a class member who took no significant part in the class action may be bound is a major step beyond the cases previously discussed in this section, since the representation of one class member by another is seldom a result of any pre-existing legal relationship. Instead, the class often comes into existence as a group only as a result of the incident giving rise to the litigation, and the class members have little or no knowledge of each other, or any interests in common, aside from those they share in the subject matter of the litigation. Indeed, in some cases, especially those involving the claim of injury resulting from the alleged "mass tort" of distributing and marketing an unreasonably unsafe product,[16] the membership of the class may run into the millions, and the location of the

16. Examples include class claims arising from harm allegedly incurred by use of, or exposure to, cigarettes, asbestos, certain

members is likely to be as widespread as the distribution of the product claimed to have caused harm. Moreover, some class members may have suffered exposure to the product, directly or indirectly, but may not yet know of any injury incurred as a result. Some may even be unborn.

Under these circumstances, any binding effect of the judgment on "absent" class members is best grounded on two factors: (a) the interests of fairness and efficiency that are served by such a result, *and* (b) the special precautions that are required to protect the interests of absent members.

On the first of these factors, the interests served are, I believe, both procedural and substantive. Procedurally, in a class that is of sufficient size and whose members have enough in common to warrant class action treatment, the economies of scale that result from disposition of the common elements should be clear—in a case in which the alternative is an indefinite number of separate actions dealing with the same issues.[17] (A different justification supports the use of the class action in cases in which each class member's claim is so small that even one individual action is unlikely to be brought. In such instances, the availability of the class action technique—though it may facilitate some actions

diet pills, Agent Orange (a defoliant used during the Vietnam War), silicone breast implants, HIV-contaminated blood, and a broad range of other products.

17. Some of these economies may also be available in related individual actions, if the lawyers and parties involved are willing and able to agree on such steps as the pooling of resources and sharing of information.

that do not increase overall social welfare—is often warranted because these "small claim" class actions serve as the most effective deterrent to unlawful conduct that would cause considerable aggregate loss to society. In other words, a technique that makes it economically feasible for lawyers to bring suit operates to put the market to work in the furtherance of the public interest.) Substantively, I and others have written of the extent to which class action treatment in a variety of cases can contribute to a new and better understanding of the rights of, and duties owed to, a class, as well of the optimal methods of allocating both the benefits of costs of litigation.[18]

On the second factor—adequate protection of the members of the class—the courts have recognized, both by rule and by application of the requirements of due process itself, that such protection is a *sine qua non* for permitting a determination to have binding effect. Thus in the federal courts and in most states, the rules of procedure governing class actions require as conditions for certification (a) that the representative party be an "adequate" representative of the class, (b) that his claim or defense present questions of law or fact common to the class, and (c) that his claim or defense be "typical" of the claim of the class.[19] And at least in

18. *See, e.g.,* David L. Shapiro, *Class Actions: The Class as Party and Client,* 73 NOTRE DAME L. REV. 913 (1998). For a selected bibliography of articles on this topic expressing a wide range of viewpoints, see *id.* at 914–16 nn. 2–4.

19. *See* FED. R. CIV. P. 23, as well as the many state rules patterned on it.

some class actions, notice to class members and a reasonable opportunity to "opt out" must also be afforded. Moreover, no class action may be dismissed or compromised without (a) proper notice to the members of the class and (b) the approval of the court—a process that ordinarily requires a "fairness" hearing with respect to such issues as the terms of the overall disposition, the method in which the overall settlement is to be allocated, and of particular importance, the amount of lawyer's fees to be awarded.[20]

To some extent, though the boundaries are still unclear, these requirements must be satisfied in any class action, state or federal, in order to comply with the requirements of due process. Foremost among these are the requirement that representation of the absent class members be adequate throughout the litigation—a requirement that looks to such factors as the representativeness of the designated party representative, the competence and experience of the attorneys representing the class, the nature and extent of conflicts either within the class itself or confronting the attorney representing the class, and any evidence of conduct in the litigation suggesting that the interests of the

20. *See* FED. R. CIV. P. 23(e). Much has been written about the appropriate content and scope of a "fairness" hearing under Rule 23(e), and it is reported that proposals for elaboration of this provision are under consideration by the Advisory Committee on the Federal Rules of Civil Procedure. *See* 68 U.S.L.W. 2694 (2000). For extended discussion of possible changes in Rule 23(e), as well as of a more broadly-based proposal for statutory change, see Edward H. Cooper, *Aggregation and Settlement of Mass Torts,* 148 U. PA. L. REV. 1943 (2000).

class were not adequately served.[21] And the Supreme Court has also indicated that at least in some class action contexts, notice to class members and the opportunity to opt out are constitutionally required.[22]

The uncertainty attending these last two factors arises for several reasons. First, it is not clear whether the Constitution requires that notice be given to all class members whose whereabouts can be ascertained, even when the costs of notice would make the action prohibitively expensive to maintain and when the amount at stake for any individual class member is so small that notice to more than a representative group would serve little or no real purpose. In such a case, the requirements of due process may end up depriving the class that is being "protected" of any effective remedy. Second, it is not clear why or to what extent the "right to opt out" is constitutionally required if class members are adequately notified and represented, if the availability of such a right may undermine not only the utility of the class action but the interests of the class as a whole in obtaining relief, and if the case is one in which even relief to those remaining in the class will inevitably affect those who have with-

21. Still a leading decision on the necessity of adequate representation, and the barriers to such representation that may be presented by the existence of intra-class conflict, is Hansberry v. Lee, 311 U.S. 32 (1940). *See also, e.g.,* Amchem Prods., Inc. v. Windsor, 521 U.S. 591 (1997) (holding, *inter alia*, that existence of intra-class conflicts precluded class certification under Rule 23).

22. *See* Phillips Petroleum Co. v. Shutts, 472 U.S. 797, 811–12 (1985).

drawn from it. Finally, in *Phillips Petroleum Co. v. Shutts*,[23] the case in which these two requirements were articulated, the Court did so with little explanation of the scope or extent of the requirements, and in a context in which many class members were located beyond the territorial limits of the jurisdiction.

A final series of questions—and perhaps the most difficult—involves the extent to which an absent class member may avoid the preclusive effect of a judgment in a collateral proceeding—most typically one in which the member seeks to pursue a claim against the defendant that is the same as the claim disposed of in the class action. Given the very function of the rules of claim preclusion in this context, some questions, like the correctness of any determinations on the merits or the fairness of a settlement, are almost certainly beyond such collateral attack. On the other hand, the question whether adequate steps were taken to notify a particular class member of the action—to fulfill the constitutional obligation of reasonable notice—is as assuredly available here as in any subsequent action in which preclusion is sought, *supra* ch. II(A)(1). But what of the question whether the representation of the class member was adequate, or (if constitutionally required) whether the class member was given an adequate opportunity to opt out? And does it matter whether and how these issues were adjudicated by the court in the initial action (assuming

23. 472 U.S. 797 (1985).

that the class member now raising the challenge did not participate in the adjudication)?

So far, the Supreme Court has given little guidance on these matters, and the lower courts are divided.[24] To take the question of adequate representation as the central one, my own view of the matter is that while the analogy is not perfect, the question is very close to the question whether a defendant who defaults may challenge the validity of the default judgment on grounds of inadequate notice or lack of territorial jurisdiction.

In such a case, it does not matter that the court that rendered the default considered and decided the issues, even if in doing so it appointed a "representative" to argue on behalf of the absent defendant. If the condition is one that is constitutionally necessary to the validity of the judgment, it would be ironic, to say the least, if a person who did not participate could be prevented from challenging the determination in a subsequent action on the ground

24. *Compare, e.g.,* Epstein v. MCA, Inc., 179 F.3d 641 (9th Cir.), *cert. denied,* 528 U.S. 1004 (1999), *with, e.g.,* Gonzales v. Cassidy, 474 F.2d 67 (5th Cir.1973). The commentators are also divided. *Compare, e.g.,* Marcel Kahan & Linda Silberman, *The Inadequate Search for "Adequacy" in Class Actions: A Critique of Epstein v. MCA, Inc.,* 73 N.Y.U.L. REV. 765 (1998), *and* Note, 87 HARV. L. REV. 589 (1974) (favoring significant restrictions on collateral attack by absent class members on the basis of inadequate representation), *with, e.g.,* Henry Paul Monaghan, *Antisuit Injunctions and Preclusion Against Absent Nonresident Class Members,* 98 COLUM. L. REV. 1148 (1998), *and* Patrick Woolley, *The Availability of Collateral Attack for Inadequate Representation in Class Suits,* 79 TEX. L. REV. 383 (2000) (advocating availability of collateral attack by absent class members on the basis of inadequate representation).

that the issue was decided against him in his absence.

4. *Persons Represented by a Party to a Prior Action: The Frontier.* Not too long ago, the topic of persons treated as parties by virtue of "representation" would have ended with the materials in the last section. And those materials still represent the prevailing view among courts and commentators, as supported by the *Restatement.* But there has arisen in case and commentary the view that the justifications for preclusion may extend beyond the cases described above. In this view, the cause of efficiency may be better served, without undue harm to any individual interests, by recognizing other instances of "virtual representation." In such instances, the argument runs, a person may and should be treated as a party to a prior litigation—at least if the person had notice of the litigation and opportunity to come in as a party—if that person's interest was sufficiently represented by someone who was a party. Under this analysis, neither the presence of some pre-existing relationship between the prior litigant and the party to be bound, nor the safeguards required for preclusion to available against absent members of a class with respect to a class action judgment, constitute a prerequisite.

Some cases may illustrate the point. Decisions representing the traditional view—that preclusion is not available against a non-party in such a case—include *Benson and Ford, Inc. v. Wanda Petroleum*

Co.,[25] and *Hardy v. Johns–Manville Sales Corp.*[26] In the *Benson and Ford* litigation, a prior antitrust suit brought by a different plaintiff (Shelby)—a suit in which Mr. Ford himself had testified as a witness—had ended in a judgment for the defendants. Benson and Ford, Inc., which had not been a party to Shelby's action, retained the same lawyer who had represented Shelby and, relying on essentially the same allegations, brought a second antitrust action against the same defendants. The court rejected the defense of preclusion, saying that Benson and Ford, Inc., did not have "control" of the initial action, that it had no duty to intervene in the prior case, and that the company had a "due process right to be heard."[27] In *Hardy*, the court similarly rejected an assertion of preclusion against some 14 defendants in an action for injuries resulting from exposure to asbestos. The defendants had not been parties to a prior action in which certain issues common to both cases had been decided against other defendants, in which the same attorneys were representing the defense, and of which the present defendants had knowledge. The court, in denying preclusion, argued that the absence of a legal relationship between the first set of defendants and the present set was a critical factor.

Two decisions representing a different view are

25. 833 F.2d 1172 (5th Cir.1987).

26. 681 F.2d 334 (5th Cir.1982). For another similar, and more recent, holding, see Tice v. American Airlines, Inc., 162 F.3d 966, 974 (7th Cir.1998), *cert. denied,* 527 U.S. 1036 (1999).

27. 833 F.2d at 1174, 1176.

Tyus v. Schoemehl,[28] and *Cauefield v. Fidelity and Casualty Co.*[29] In *Cauefield*, a case claiming injury based on grave desecration, a federal action was stayed while a state action by a different plaintiff went forward, and after the defendant prevailed in the state court, the federal action was dismissed.[30] In *Tyus*, perhaps the most extreme example of the "new frontier," the plaintiffs in the first action unsuccessfully attacked the validity of certain district boundaries drawn by the defendant (a government officer), and the court held that a second action making the same claim was precluded, even with respect to plaintiffs who were not parties to the first suit. The court specifically relied on a "virtual representation" theory, and stressed that for this theory to be available, there must be some "special relationship" between the parties in the two actions. But, the court contended, such a relationship could exist despite the lack of any express or implied "legal" relation (such as those mentioned in section A, above).[31]

28.   93 F.3d 449 (8th Cir.1996).

29.   378 F.2d 876 (5th Cir.), *cert. denied,* 389 U.S. 1009 (1967). *Cf.* Aerojet–General Corp. v. Askew, 511 F.2d 710 (5th Cir.), *cert. denied,* 423 U.S. 908 (1975) (defendant county precluded by judgment entered against defendant state agencies).

30.   378 F.2d at 879. The Reporter's Note to RSJ § 62 disapproves of the *Cauefield* result. In *Benson and Ford, Cauefield* was distinguished—by the court that decided it—on the (questionable) ground that in *Cauefield* there was a "tacit agreement" to abide by the result in the state court action. 833 F.2d at 1175–76.

31.   93 F.2d at 455. For a decision falling somewhere in between, see Southwest Airlines Co. v. Texas Int'l Airlines, 546

Commentators, like courts, have expressed a range of views on this question.[32] Some have vigorously defended the traditional view, some have advocated a considerable expansion of the reach of

F.2d 84 (5th Cir.1977). In that case, the city of Dallas, relying on a city ordinance, had sued in federal court to prevent Southwest from using the Love Field airport, and had lost. A second action, seeking the same relief, was then brought against the airline in state court by several airlines that had known of, and whose representatives had sat in at, the first proceeding. The second action was enjoined by the federal court, and as the decision was later explained by the same court in *Benson and Ford*: "Our holding rested on the proposition that private parties cannot relitigate to enforce an ordinance after the public body fails in its attempt to enforce the same ordinance." 833 F.2d at 1176.

32. *Compare, e.g.,* Pielemeier, *supra* note 1, at 431–35 (advocating a limited application of preclusion against non-parties), *and* Howard M. Erichson, *Informal Aggregation: Procedural and Ethical Implications of Coordination Among Counsel in Related Lawsuits,* 50 DUKE L.J. 381, 458 (2000) (opposing non-party preclusion based on coordination of the non-party's counsel and counsel for another in a prior suit because such preclusion "would create disincentives to counsel coordination" and would make it possible to circumvent such formal protections of absent parties as those built into the class action rule); *with, e.g.,* Robert G. Bone, *Rethinking the "Day in Court" Ideal and Nonparty Preclusion,* 67 N.Y.U.L. REV. 193 (1992) (advocating a greater willingness to apply preclusion rules against non-parties), *and* Michael A. Berch, *A Proposal to Permit Collateral Estoppel of Nonparties Seeking Affirmative Relief,* 1979 ARIZ. ST. L.J. 511 (same). For a comprehensive discussion and citation of other authorities, see JAY TIDMARSH & ROGER H. TRANSGRUD, COMPLEX LITIGATION AND THE ADVERSARY SYSTEM ch. 2 (1998); *id.* Supp. 2000, at 11–14.

Those commentators who advocate a broader approach to binding non-parties do not necessarily limit their arguments to instances of what courts have viewed as "virtual representation" by one who was a party in the prior proceeding, *see, e.g.,* Berch, *supra,* at 533, and thus those arguments are also relevant to the issues considered in the next section.

preclusion, and some have indicated that a "broader" approach may be appropriate in "public law litigation" (like *Tyus*), in order to prevent endless pursuit of the same claim against a public institution. And very much in the foreground, setting some constitutional limits to the demarcation of the frontier, are several Supreme Court decisions making it clear that the assertion of preclusion against a non-party will frequently run afoul of the requirements of due process.[33]

If law, as Holmes argued, is the prediction of what the judges will do, the "law" in this field is certainly not easy to state, and in any event I have

---

33. *See, e.g.,* Richards v. Jefferson County, Alabama, 517 U.S. 793 (1996), in which the loss of a state court suit brought by certain taxpayers to establish the invalidity of a tax was held (on due process grounds) not to preclude an identical state court challenge by other taxpayers. *See also, e.g.,* Baker v. General Motors Corp., 522 U.S. 222 (1998) (holding a non-party not bound by a state court injunction prohibiting a person from giving certain testimony in any judicial proceeding).

In neither *Richards* nor *Baker* did it appear that the non-party in question had adequate notice of the initial proceeding. But in South Central Bell Tel. Co. v. Alabama, 119 S.Ct. 1180 (1999), the Court went out of its way to apply the *Richards* rationale in a context in which the non-parties to the first action were aware of that action and were represented by one of the same lawyers who represented the plaintiffs in the first action. In holding that the state court could not bar the second action on preclusion grounds, the Court first acknowledged the state's decision *not* to rely on an assertion of preclusion and then went on to reject the assertion that had not been made. The facts described above, the Court said, "created no special representational relationship between the earlier and later plaintiffs. Nor could these facts have led the later plaintiffs to expect to be precluded, as a matter of res judicata, by the earlier judgment itself.... " *Id.* at 1185.

always thought that Holmes' definition is of little value to judges, since it would require them to predict what they will do.

My own view, however, is that this new frontier should be carefully guarded against expansion. In the first place, both the impact of stare decisis and the human tendency not to waste money will deter the bringing of suits based on claims or issues that have already been adversely determined against others. And second, defendants fearing a multiplicity of suits by a series of plaintiffs have available to them, in many instances, such devices as defensive use of a class action or other techniques of mandatory joinder. Third, unlike the class action, the use of preclusion against the non-participant in the first case is not hedged in by procedural safeguards designed to insure protection of the absent person's interests. And finally, for the reasons just stated, combined with our firm belief in the value of litigant autonomy (including the choice of the time and place to sue), considerations of due process do set limits to expansion of the frontier.

B. Other Non–parties

---

1. *When, If Ever, May a Non–party Not Within the Scope of III(A) Be Burdened By the Preclusive Effect of a Prior Judgment*? The limits of the concept of being treated "as a party" may not even end with the concept of "virtual representation." The term itself has an aura of fiction about it that makes it in some respects hard to distinguish from

the cases discussed in the present section, and indeed some of the cases already discussed might fit easily into this section as well. The question now on the table is whether, wholly apart from the question whether a non-party was "represented" by a party to a prior litigation, there are situations when considerations of efficiency warrant, and considerations of fairness do not prohibit, the imposition of the burdens of the rules of preclusion (including claim preclusion) on that non-party. More specifically, are there instances in which a non-party may be allowed to suffer the pain of preclusion on the ground that the person had timely notice of the action and a reasonable opportunity to intervene?[34]

34. The provisions of the *Restatement (Second)* adhere to the more traditional view on this issue, providing for the burdening of a third person (other than in the instances already discussed in Section A) only in two situations. The first (RSJ § 62) provides that such a person may be precluded from asserting a claim arising out of a transaction that was the subject of a prior action if (a) the claimant knew about the prior action before judgment, (b) enforcement of the claim would result in imposing inconsistent obligations on the original defendant or would otherwise severely prejudice that defendant, *and* (c) the claimant had acted in a way that induced the original defendant to believe that the claimant would be governed by the first judgment or for some other reason would forgo procedures that could have resolved the claim in the first action. These conditions will rarely be satisfied, and represent a much narrower scope of preclusion than some versions discussed during the process of drafting the *Restatement* provision. The second situation (dealt with in RSJ § 63) is discussed in Section B(3), below.

In a later ALI project, however, a more adventurous step was proposed: that a statute be enacted providing that, in complex litigation, a non-party who has a claim closely related to a pending action, who is properly notified, and who is within the

The problem may be illustrated by the Supreme Court's decision in *Martin v. Wilks*[35] and its legislative aftermath. In this Title VII case,[36] after preliminary litigation with a class representing minority firefighters, a municipal fire department had entered into a consent decree with the class providing, *inter alia*, for a schedule of promotions within the department. After the approval of that decree by the court, an action was brought against the department by white firefighters, claiming that the decree violated their rights not to be discriminated against. The defendant's plea of preclusion was rejected by the Supreme Court, and the Court explicitly stated that the failure of the white firefighters to intervene in the prior action could not serve as the basis of preclusion of their separate suit. In its decision the Court referred to the principle that one is not bound by a judgment in a litigation in which he is not made a party as "part of our 'deep-rooted historic tradition that everyone should have his own day in court.' "[37] But the Court's holding did not rest on constitutional grounds; rather it relied on

court's territorial jurisdiction "may intervene in the action and *in any event* will be bound by the determinations made [i.e., subject to issue preclusion] to the same extent as a party, unless otherwise provided by law." AMERICAN LAW INSTITUTE, COMPLEX LITIGATION: STATUTORY RECOMMENDATIONS AND ANALYSIS § 5.05(a) (1994) (emphasis added).

35. 490 U.S. 755 (1989).

36. Title VII of the Civil Rights Act of 1964, as amended, 42 U.S.C. §§ 2000e *et seq.*

37. 490 U.S. at 762 (quoting 18 CHARLES A. WRIGHT, ARTHUR R. MILLER & EDWARD H. COOPER, FEDERAL PRACTICE AND PROCEDURE § 4449, at 417 (1981)).

its interpretation of the federal rule governing intervention (Rule 24) as permissive, not mandatory and added its own agreement that the "burden of bringing in additional parties" should rest on those already parties to the litigation.[38]

This decision was one of several in the civil rights area that led to the Civil Rights Act of 1991.[39] In response to the decision in *Martin*, Congress provided that in Title VII cases, a person would be precluded from attacking a judgment (a) if his interests were adequately represented by a person who had already attacked the judgment, *or* (b) if, prior to the entry of judgment, the person had received "actual notice" of the proposed judgment and its possible adverse effect and had been afforded "a reasonable opportunity to present objections to such judgment." But, mindful of the possible constitutional problems with such a provision, Congress inserted the (superfluous) clause that the provision was effective only to the extent permitted by the Constitution.

Some support for the constitutionality of this provision may be found in the rather cryptic dictum of the Supreme Court in a 1968 decision, *Provident Tradesmens Bank & Trust Co. v. Patterson*.[40] In that case, the Court said that a non-party who "purposefully bypassed an adequate opportunity to intervene" might suffer the consequences of preclusion as a result of the judgment. But to a significant

38. 490 U.S. at 765.

39. 42 U.S.C. § 2000e–2(n)(1).

40. 390 U.S. 102, 114 (1968).

extent, the decisions in the *Richards, Baker,* and *South Central Bell* cases (*see supra* note 33) have limited the implications of that thought.

Two questions are presented by the *Martin* decision and its aftermath. First, should the courts take it upon themselves to develop a doctrine of preclusion along these lines, or should they continue, as in *Martin* itself, to resist pressures to do so? My own view is that they should continue to resist. Deep-seated traditions of litigant autonomy, long-accepted limitations on the scope of preclusion, and the dangers of binding those who had good reason for staying out of a lawsuit that was not litigated either with their interests in mind or (in the case of a class action) in the presence of elaborate safeguards designed to protect those interests—all these factors militate in favor of caution in extending the doctrine of preclusion this far.

Assuming that this view is sound, the question remains whether the legislature may constitutionally decide, at least in specific contexts, that preclusion is warranted in a case like the one described in the statutory provision overruling *Martin*. In my view, it may—if the provision for preclusion is accompanied by adequate safeguards of notice and opportunity to participate.[41] After all, in many

41. Even in South Central Bell Tel. Co. v. Alabama, 526 U.S. 160 (1999) (discussed *supra* note 33), which suggests perhaps the broadest scope of due process protection against preclusion, the Supreme Court stressed that the non-party had an insufficient basis "to expect to be precluded, as a matter of res judicata." *Id.* at 168. The provisions of the 1991 Civil Rights Act, discussed in

cases, what is principally at issue is the location of
the burden of joinder: does it rest on one who is
already a party or does it rest on the outsider who
knows (or should know) of the action? In this context, adequate notice and reasonable opportunity to
participate in the initial action seem to me to satisfy
the threshold requirements of due process. Thus,
the appropriateness (sadly, often honored in the
breach these days) of deference to the judgments of
the legislative, politically responsible branch should
serve to sustain the validity of properly framed
statutory exceptions to the prevailing common law
rule.

2. *When May a Non–party Not Within the Scope of III(A) Receive the Benefits of the Preclusive Effect of a Prior Judgment?*

Until relatively recently (roughly the period between the two World Wars), it was part of the
received—though sometimes criticized—learning
that one could not obtain any of the benefits of the
rules of preclusion unless one could also be saddled
with the burdens. And this rule of "mutuality"
meant that the benefits of preclusion doctrine were
available only to those who were either parties to
the prior litigation (as defined in Chapter II(E)), or
persons to be treated as parties (as defined in the
more traditional senses described in Section A of
this Chapter). But the story of the last 60 years or
so in the world of preclusion has been the story of

text, and of the proposed statute discussed *supra* note 34, appear
to furnish just such a basis.

the gradual erosion of the mutuality rule—followed more recently by second thoughts about whether the erosion is sufficiently justified. That story is the subject of this section.

(a) *Claim Preclusion*. Unlike the dramatic retreat from mutuality that has occurred with respect to issue preclusion (discussed below), the traditional approach to claim preclusion—that one may not benefit by it unless one is also bound by it—has persisted in most jurisdictions. Thus, to revert, after a long hiatus, to the hypothetical of The Accident (*supra* p. 22), if A sues B for negligence and loses on a ground having no issue preclusive consequences for future litigation—say, failure to prosecute—A will not be barred by the rules of claim preclusion from suing C for harm resulting from the same accident. The logic of this result is impeccable: whether or not a claim is defined in terms of the transaction that gave rise to it, A's claim against C is not the same as A's claim against B, just as B's counterclaim against A is different from A's original claim.

But whether logical or not, the wisdom of the result is debatable. In its favor as a matter of policy, it can be argued that A should be able to choose her targets selectively if she wishes. After all, if she brings successive suits in the example just given, neither of her adversaries is being required to litigate the controversy more than once. Moreover, statutes of limitations—generally short in tort cases—are designed to prevent such controversies from being brought to court long after their occurrence. And allowing B to assert claim preclusion in the second action may compel A to overlitigate the first case by suing multiple defendants and thus exposing herself to a far more costly process. Assuming that A will pick the "best" defendant (from her point of view) to sue first, allowing successive suits may actually decrease both the quantity and the cost of litigation.

Yet the arguments for a kind of "compulsory joinder" in cases involving multiple defendants and the same transaction are not without force. Whenever the same incident gives rise to more than one lawsuit, the cost to the judicial system itself is significant in view of the economies of scale. And if A does join all available defendants in one suit (*i.e.*, those who can be joined under the applicable rules of territorial jurisdiction and venue), A is at least as likely as not to benefit from the efforts of each defendant to pin the blame on the other(s).

Only one jurisdiction, New Jersey, accepted this view by adopting what has come to be called "the entire controversy doctrine,"[42] and another, Kansas, adopted it in the context of cases involving issues of comparative negligence.[43] But the doctrine has excited academic interest, and some support. Indeed, one commentator argued forcefully that an inroad

42. *See* Cogdell v. Hospital Ctr., 560 A.2d 1169 (N.J.1989). The *Cogdell* decision and its progeny were the subject of a symposium in 28 Rutgers L.J. 1 (1996).

43. *See, e.g.,* Mick v. Mani, 766 P.2d 147 (Kan.1988). The Kansas rule is sometimes described as the "one action" or "one trial" rule. *Id.* at 158.

on mutuality in this respect—at least to the extent of claims against multiple defendants arising out of the same event—has more to be said for it than some of the more widely accepted inroads that have occurred with respect to issue preclusion.[44] In my view, however one comes out on the need for mutuality with respect to issue preclusion, the case for a "requirement" of multiple joinder—for telling a plaintiff that she must either join all the defendants who can reasonably be joined with respect to a particular transaction or forgo a future claim against those not joined—is not without merit. But after weighing the costs and benefits, New Jersey itself decided to revise its rules of practice in 1998 to eliminate the doctrine except in special situations involving both inexcusable conduct and substantial prejudice.

(b) *Issue Preclusion*. The evolution of judicial and scholarly attitudes toward the problem of "nonmutual issue preclusion"—allowing a non-party to a prior action to claim the benefits of issue preclusion with respect to determinations made in that action—can be described at great length, but I will try to be reasonably brief. And to help the story along, let me pose two variations based on the hypothetical of The Accident: (1) A sues B for negligence, and after trial, loses on the express ground that A's contributory negligence was the sole cause of the accident. A then sues C (in any of the vast majority

44. *See* Michael J. Waggoner, *Fifty Years of* Bernhard v. Bank of America *Is Enough: Collateral Estoppel Should Require Mutuality But Res Judicata Should Not,* 12 Rᴇᴠ. Lɪᴛɪɢ. 391 (1993).

of states that do not hold A barred by the doctrine of claim preclusion), and C relies on the defense that A's sole responsibility for the accident has already been determined. (2) Same outcome in the first case, but in the second action, C sues A for the harms resulting from the accident and relies on issue preclusion to establish A's legal responsibility for the accident.

In a further effort to make discussion easier (or at least a bit shorter), I have coined some unpronounceable acronyms. Both hypotheticals raise the problem of "non-mutual issue preclusion," or NMIP—the availability of issue preclusion to one who was not a party, or to be treated as a party, to the first litigation. The first hypothetical involves the *defensive* use of non-mutual issue preclusion (NMDIP) by the non-party (C), and the second involves the *offensive* use of non-mutual issue preclusion (NMOIP) by C.[45]

Until the middle of the twentieth century, NMIP would not have been available to C in either situation, because the rule of mutuality reigned in all, or virtually all, American jurisdictions. One exception that was recognized during this period involved what has been called the "indemnity anomaly." This anomaly was presented when in Action No. 1,

45. Waggoner, *supra* note 44, at 405, 408, would divide the relevant categories not into "defensive" and "offensive" but into "mono-claims" and "poly-claims" (the former involving claims arising out of the same transaction and the latter claims arising out of different transactions). But I don't believe that division is as useful, at least for dealing with the law as it has developed.

A sued B and lost and then in action No. 2, A sued C with respect to the same transaction but based the claim against C solely on a theory of derivative liability—a theory (respondeat superior, for example) that made C liable for B's wrong but at the same time gave C a right of indemnification against B in the event that C was held liable and required to pay a judgment. In that case, if A were permitted to proceed against C and to prevail, either C would be entitled to indemnification from B, which would effectively nullify B's victory, or C would be denied indemnification, which would sustain B's victory but deprive C of his legal right. The solution was to bar A's action against C, and indeed the need to avoid the anomaly was viewed as sufficiently strong that this bar was sometimes viewed as a matter not just of issue preclusion but of claim preclusion; B's victory in the first action, in other words, was not to be undone. And the application of preclusion in this situation was recognized in the *Restatement (First)*, published in 1942.[46]

To abbreviate developments following recognition of the indemnity anomaly, a major shift in thinking was marked by the decision in *Bernhard v. Bank of America*,[47] a case in which, on its facts, application of the existing indemnity rule would have served to protect the second defendant from having to litigate against a plaintiff who had lost the initial action.

46. RESTATEMENT (FIRST) OF JUDGMENTS §§ 96–98 (1942). *Cf. id.* § 99 ("Where liability of a person is based solely upon the act of another").

47. 122 P.2d 892 (Cal.1942).

But Justice Traynor, writing for the court, decided to venture a good deal further. After all, he reasoned, if the plaintiff had failed to prevail on an issue on which she had had a full and fair opportunity to litigate, what value to the litigants or to the judicial system would be served by allowing the plaintiff to litigate the issue again, and in doing so, to impose potentially heavy costs on the new adversary and on the courts? In short, issue preclusion should be available to the non-party, in his view, under essentially the same circumstances that it would be available to a party (or one treated as a party) in accordance with the rules discussed in Chapter II and Section A of this Chapter.

Bernhard itself involved NMDIP, and the case for the *Bernhard* result seems strongest in that context. At least in the absence of a requirement of compulsory joinder, one effect of NMDIP is to put pressure on the plaintiff to join all defendants who can be joined in the initial action, thus saving the costs of several adjudications of similar or identical issues. Admittedly, this pressure is most significant when the second action arises out of the same transaction as the first, though joinder may be available even when it does not.[48] And in any event, the majority of cases raising the possibility of

48. The availability of joinder depends on the scope of permissible joinder under the forum's procedural rules. Under FED. R. CIV. P. 20(a), joinder of additional persons as plaintiffs or defendants is limited to cases involving claims "arising out of the same transaction, occurrence, or series of transactions or occurrences *and* if any question of law or fact common to all [these persons] will arise in the action" (emphasis added).

NMDIP do, I suspect, involve the same or closely related transactions. Moreover, the benefits of allowing relitigation in such a case do not seem substantial.

Considerable impetus was given to the changes set in motion by Justice Traynor when the Supreme Court in 1971, in *Blonder-Tongue Laboratories, Inc. v. University of Illinois Foundation*,[49] applied NMDIP in a case involving a second action for alleged patent infringement by a plaintiff who had lost an earlier infringement action against another defendant on the ground that the patent sued on was invalid. The Court discussed the policy factors favoring preclusion, stressing that the plaintiff had had an adequate opportunity and incentive to litigate the issue of validity in the first proceeding. While the Supreme Court's decision was rendered in the context of the litigation of federal claims in the federal courts, and did not purport to bind the states, the Court's lead was followed by many states and by the *Restatement (Second)* (RSJ § 29).

Some eight years later, in *Parklane Hosiery Co. v. Shore*,[50] the Supreme Court dealt with the more difficult problem of NMOIP. In *Parklane*, the Securities and Exchange Commission had obtained a federal court injunction against the continuation of certain practices by the defendant; in a subsequent federal court damages action brought by a private plaintiff against the same defendant and based on the same alleged violations, the plaintiff sought to

49. 402 U.S. 313 (1971).
50. 439 U.S. 322 (1979).

establish the violations by relying on NMOIP. The Supreme Court, while recognizing that the case for issue preclusion was not as strong as in the defensive context, nevertheless allowed preclusion to be used as a sword. At the same time, it insisted that before allowing such use, the court should be assured that there were no reasons of policy, or of fairness to the party to be precluded, cutting against preclusion. One significant factor—not present in *Parklane*—was referred to by the Court as weighing against preclusion in such a case: that the party asserting it had passed up a reasonable opportunity to participate in the initial action. Another factor that was present in *Parklane* did not deter the majority from according preclusive effect to the first decision: that the defendant had a constitutional right to a jury in the second action for damages but not in the first action for equitable relief.[51] Although the state courts continue to be divided on the problem presented in *Parklane*, many courts agree with the analysis in that case, as does the *Restatement (Second)* (RSJ § 29).[52]

During this period, the enthusiasm for NMIP has been far from universal. Some courts and observers have opposed it entirely, while others have empha-

51. This aspect of *Parklane* was later qualified in Lytle v. Household Mfg., 494 U.S. 545 (1990), in which the Court held that a party that had been *erroneously* denied a jury trial on an issue in a prior proceeding was entitled to a jury trial of that issue in a subsequent proceeding.

52. For a survey of state court decisions as of 1982, see the Reporter's Note to RSJ § 29. *See also* authorities cited in Howard M. Erichson, *Interjurisdictional Preclusion*, 96 MICH. L. REV. 945, 965–69 (1998).

sized the importance of recognizing certain limitations and/or of careful examination of the particular circumstances to make sure that its use is justified.

Broad arguments against any use of NMIP can be and have been made on a number of grounds.[53] For example, it can be forcefully contended that the very idea of NMIP rests on the false premise that an "issue" can exist "in the air," when in truth issues (at least of fact and perhaps of law as well) always arise in the context of a particular controversy between particular adversaries. Thus, a determination in the matter of The Accident that harm to B resulted from wrongful conduct by A may have rested on such factors as the nature of B's injuries; the impression that B made on the trier of fact, and the relative depths of the pockets of A and B. None of these factors has much to do with the question whether A's conduct in the same transaction should render A liable to C.

Also, the potential application of NMIP—in the view of some observers—creates an undesirable distortion in the stakes of the two parties to the initial controversy. To take an extreme case, if thousands claim injury from a single defendant's course of conduct, and one of the allegedly injured brings suit, the defendant's loss (if NMOIP is allowed) will

53. A leading opponent of the use of NMIP is Waggoner, *supra* note 44. But as stated above, Waggoner strongly favors the ability of a non-party to assert *claim* preclusion as a defense in a subsequent action arising out of the same transaction or occurrence as a prior suit in which he could have been, but was not, joined as a defendant. *See also, e.g.,* Note, 76 MICH. L. REV. 612 (1978).

subject it to liability not only to the plaintiff but to all the others who claim a similar injury, while the plaintiff has nothing to lose but the case at hand. This distortion may either lead the defendant to invest disproportionately in the first case in order to prevail and to prevent NMIP—with a corresponding loss of efficiency and prejudice to the plaintiff—or give the plaintiff more leverage in negotiating a settlement than he would otherwise have had because a settlement will not have any future issue preclusive effect.

Finally, the use of NMIP has the effect of saving the non-party to the first action the cost of litigating the issue even once—a saving that seems broader than warranted by the rationale underlying the doctrine (*supra* pp. 11–18)—while barring the adverse party from *re*litigating even though he would be happy to incur the additional costs.

Narrower arguments attack particular aspects of the concept of NMIP. For example, it has been suggested that the public interest may militate in favor of relitigation. This argument has special force with regard to issues of law when the losing party in the first case is the government itself, because NMIP may foreclose the highest court in the jurisdiction from ever deciding the issue unless the government seeks to appeal its first defeat; thus NMIP in this case may pressure the highest court to accept such appeals—even where its appellate jurisdiction is discretionary—rather than wait to see how other lower courts deal with the issue.

Another argument focused on the undesirability of offensive use of issue preclusion begins by conceding that NMDIP may in many instances induce a plaintiff to *join* all potential defendants in one action—a decision that would tend to increase judicial efficiency if the alternative is a series of separate suits brought individually against each defendant.[54] But, the argument continues, NMOIP is likely to induce potential plaintiffs *not to join* in an existing litigation because of the rewards of a "wait and see" posture. If the plaintiff wins, other plaintiffs can ride to success on his coattails; if the plaintiff loses, those same people are free to try to prevail on their own.

Ironically, then, the rule of mutuality—a rule once thought to have been born in excessively formalistic reasoning and to have outlived any usefulness it may ever have had—now finds more sophisticated and eloquent defenders in some or all of its aspects. And partly as a result of these arguments, some jurisdictions have chosen to retain the rule, some have chosen to limit NMIP to defensive use, and those that have adopted both NMDIP and NMOIP almost universally recognize that the new approach must be applied with care.

54. The statement needs to be qualified, however, since in the absence of a strong inducement to join all defendants, the plaintiff may select only the best target for the initial action. If the suit is successful, the plaintiff may recover all of his damages from that defendant, rendering any subsequent suits unnecessary; and if the suit is unsuccessful, plaintiff may choose not to throw good money after bad by suing another.

Many of these limitations and safeguards appear in the text or commentary of Section 29 of the *Restatement (Second)*, and are reflected in judicial decisions. Not only does this section reiterate the safeguards normally recognized when the second action is between the same parties (see RSJ § 28), but it also emphasizes the relevance of such factors as (1) the presence in the second action of significant new procedural opportunities,[55] (2) the failure of the person asserting NMIP to take advantage of a reasonable opportunity to participate in the first action,[56] (3) the public interest in allowing a second determination,[57] (4) an inconsistency between the

55. This factor, and others, were alluded to by the Court in the *Parklane* decision. *See* 439 U.S. at 330–31.

56. This factor was emphasized in *Parklane*, *see* 439 U.S. at 332, but the extent to which lower courts have overlooked or disregarded it is documented in Jack Ratliff, *Offensive Collateral Estoppel and the Option Effect,* 67 Texas L. Rev. 63, 84–87 (1988)

57. This factor has proved especially significant in deciding whether to apply NMIP, and especially NMOIP, against the federal government. *See* United States v. Mendoza, 464 U.S. 154 (1984), in which the Court, holding the federal government not precluded from relitigating an issue of law that it had lost against a prior litigant, emphasized the factors noted above, p. 112, *i.e.,* the public interest in allowing the government to litigate the same issue in several lower courts in order to allow fuller consideration of the issue and to see whether a conflict of lower court decisions would develop that warranted Supreme Court discretionary review.

A question raised by *Mendoza*, however, has caused considerable controversy: the extent to which the rationale of that decision warrants the executive branch in refusing to acquiesce in a circuit court decision even with respect to matters that are sure to come before the same circuit court on judicial review. *See* HART & WECHSLER, *supra* note 6, at 1481–84, and authorities there cited. Another important question is the extent to which the

determination relied on and a determination in an earlier action,[58] (5) a significant difference in the relationships between the parties in the two actions, and (6) special circumstances, such as the availability now (but not before) of a critical witness.

The advantages and disadvantages of NMIP are surely difficult to balance. And it may well be that the many factors requiring consideration if NMIP is not to be abused mean that, in any event, the game is not worth the candle. But my own view—based on consideration of the arguments pro and con and on some educated guesses about the rules in operation, but not on solid empirical data—is that the virtues of NMIP exceed the defects so long as the limitations are marked with sufficient clarity and uniformly applied by all tribunals within the jurisdiction. The costs and delays of litigation are harsh enough; if we can achieve a measure of efficiency while preserving the core of procedural fairness to

rationale of *Mendoza* applies to *state* governments. *See* Note, 109 HARV. L. REV. 792, 808–09 (1996) (arguing that NMIP should be presumptively unavailable against state government unless application of a multi-factor balancing test overcomes the presumption).

58. If this factor is given weight, it will alleviate the problem of the "extreme" case of multiple injuries discussed in text, *supra* pp. 111–12. But it does not fully resolve that problem, since the defendant's overall risk (potential liability to others if the case is lost) is still a disproportionate one. This disparity suggests the virtues of class action treatment in a case involving multiple plaintiffs injured as a result of a shared event, transaction, or series of related transactions. For a forceful argument that the class action approach is, in general, preferable to an abandonment of mutuality in non-class action litigation, see Ratliff, *supra* note 56.

all, we can to some extent alleviate the burden on litigants and the public. And one factor often overlooked is the effect of a strong preclusion rule in deterring unnecessary litigation. If every party threatened with NMIP were to contest its application to the hilt, there might well be a net loss of social welfare. But that seems unlikely if litigants act with a reasonable degree of rationality and the outcome is sufficiently predictable.

3. *The Practical Impact of a Judgment on Non–parties.* In human affairs, events occur that inevitably affect non-participants in those events, and the realm of litigation is no exception. The *Restatement (First)* explicitly recognized this in a section entitled "Existence of a judgment as an operative fact" (§ 111), and while no precise equivalent exists in the *Restatement (Second)*—perhaps because the matter is not strictly one of the scope of the rules of "preclusion"—the proposition is no less true because of its omission.

Several examples may be useful. First, some injunctive decrees will inevitability affect persons who are neither parties themselves nor (in the absence of a properly certified class action) represented by parties. For example, a student who is an individual plaintiff in a challenge to the constitutionality of an allegedly segregated school system may obtain injunctive relief that affects many or all other students in the system.

Second, a decree may itself have, or may lead to, a "transformational" effect that affects those not parties.[59] One clear instance: a defendant complies with a judicial order to convey certain real property to the plaintiff; once the property has been conveyed, the defendant is no longer in a position to convey it to another, either voluntarily or in response to a judicial decree. And another example: after a court with the necessary jurisdiction grants a divorce to a previously married couple, a third person is not in a position to claim that the couple is still married.

Third, a judgment may create in others a duty not to obstruct compliance. The *Restatement* (RSJ § 63 cmt. a, illus. 2) gives as an illustration of this duty a case in which, after a plaintiff obtains a money judgment from a defendant, the defendant attempts to avoid enforcement by conveying his assets to a third person. If the third person knew or had reason to know of the fraud, the property can be reached by the judgment creditor without giving the third person an opportunity to contest the first judgment on the merits.

In recognition of these potential effects of a judgment on strangers to the action, the *Restatement* (RSJ § 76) provides that a person not bound by the rules of preclusion may nevertheless be able to bring an action to protect his interests. Thus, if P asserts that he has a contract to purchase certain property from A, and a court has entered a judgment ordering A to convey that property to B (who has no knowledge or notice of the contract of sale to

59. The term in quotes is used in FLEMING JAMES, JR., GEOFFREY C. HAZARD, JR. & JOHN LEUBSDORF, CIVIL PROCEDURE § 11.24 (4th ed. 1992).

P), P may be able to bring an action to set aside the judgment in favor of B.

CHAPTER IV

INTERJURISDICTIONAL PRECLUSION

Introduction

To this point, we have been assuming that both the initial action and the later action in which a question of preclusion is raised are brought in the same jurisdiction—usually the same state of the United States.[1] In this chapter, we add the complication that the later action is brought in a different jurisdiction (F–2), whose rules of preclusion may differ from those of the first (F–1).

The discussion here looks first to the case in which F–1 is a state of the United States and F–2 is a sister state. Then it turns to the case in which F–1 is a state court and F–2 is a federal court, and follows with the converse problem in which F–1 is federal and F–2 is state.[2] The discussion concludes with our first and only venture into the international sphere, and focuses on the case in which F–1 is in

1. Some special problems, discussed in Section C(2) of this chapter, may arise when both actions are brought in federal court, especially if subject matter jurisdiction in the first action was based not on federal substantive law but on diversity of citizenship. But in general, the discussion in Chapters II and III is equally relevant to successive actions in the federal courts.

2. A brief subsection, referred to in note 1, *supra*, addresses the situation in which both F–1 and F–2 are federal courts.

a foreign country and F–2 is a court (state or federal) in the United States. This last topic is one of burgeoning importance as a result both of the ease and frequency of international travel and communication and of the globalization of the economy. It is the continuing subject of protracted and difficult negotiations in which this country has been a major participant.

Even more than in previous chapters, it is critical to distinguish between questions of the "recognition" of judgments—questions clustering around the concepts of claim and issue preclusion—and questions of "enforcement." To the extent these questions overlap—and they often do–the discussion of recognition will bear on matters of enforceability, but a number of enforcement issues do lie outside the scope of this study. The distinction is especially important with respect to judgments granting some form of equitable relief, since the question whether F–2 must enforce a decree granted by a court in F–1, even when both forums are within the United States, is one that continues to cause difficulty.[3] Yet such a decree, like any other judgment, will have claim and issue preclusive effects across jurisdictional lines. And even in the less uncertain realm of money judgments, the techniques of enforcement, and the time available to seek enforcement, vary among American jurisdictions.[4]

3. *See* RESTATEMENT (SECOND) OF CONFLICTS OF LAWS § 102, cmt. c (1971); Baker v. General Motors Corp., 522 U.S. 222, 235–36 (1998).

4. This variance has been held permissible–at least within reasonable limits—by the Supreme Court. *See, e.g.,* M'Elmoyle v.

A. When F–1 Is a Tribunal of One State and F–2 Is a Tribunal of a Sister State

To return to The Accident (*supra* p. 22), assume that A sues B in a state court and that the action is dismissed for failure to prosecute. Assume also that A can find another state that has territorial jurisdiction over B and files a second action on the same claim against B in that state. May A pursue the action if the preclusion rules of F–2 do not regard the first dismissal as a bar to a second action on the same claim?

If F–1 is a judicial tribunal, both the federal Constitution and a federal statutory provision enacted to implement it significantly limit F–2's discretion in such a case. Article IV, Section 1, of the Constitution (the "Full Faith and Credit Clause") provides that the "Acts, Records, and judicial Proceedings" of each state are entitled to full faith and credit in the courts of other states, and 28 U.S.C. § 1738, expanding on this text, provides that state judicial proceedings "shall have the *same* full faith and credit in *every* court within the United States . . . as they have by law or usage in the courts of such State . . . from which they are taken" (empha-

Cohen, 38 U.S. (13 Pet.) 312, 327–29 (1839); Watkins v. Conway, 385 U.S. 188, 190 (1966); Lea Brilmayer, *Credit Due Judgments and Credit Due Laws: The Respective Roles of Due Process and Full Faith and Credit in the Interstate Context*, 70 Iowa L. Rev. 95, 101–02 (1984).

sis added).[5]

Though the precise nature of a state's full faith and credit obligation is a matter of considerable controversy with respect to the *laws* of a sister state, both precedent and the terms of the implementing statute more clearly circumscribe F–2's discretion when it comes to a sister state's *judgments*.[6] Thus, in the hypothetical posed at the outset, the preclusive effect of F–1's judgment is largely determined by the law of F–1—subject to some limitations and areas of uncertainty explored more fully below. If F–1's preclusion rule provides that the dismissal of the first action bars A from suing B

5. Throughout this chapter, the discussion centers on situations in which both F–1 and F–2 are courts. If the F–1 tribunal is not a court but, say, an administrative or arbitral tribunal, neither the Constitution nor the statute is directly applicable, and F–2 clearly has broader discretion. This situation is discussed in Section B of this chapter, in the context of the preclusive effect of a state determination in a subsequent action in a federal forum.

6. In addition, Congress has enacted special provisions relating to the full faith and credit to be accorded to child custody orders (28 U.S.C. § 1738A), and to child support orders (28 U.S.C. § 1738B). Under these provisions, such orders must be given greater recognition than the Constitution itself would require, but the authority delegated to Congress under Article IV does to some undefined extent authorize such legislation. *See* Yarborough v. Yarborough, 290 U.S. 202, 215 n. 2 (1933) (Stone, J., dissenting), and authorities there cited.

In a more controversial provision, Congress has provided that "[n]o State ... shall be required to give effect to any public act, record, or judicial proceeding of any other State ... respecting a relationship between persons of the same sex that is treated as a marriage under the laws of such other State...." (28 U.S.C. § 1738C). (Query: does the power of Congress under Article IV extend to a provision allowing one state to *deny* full faith and credit to the judgment—or other public act—of another state

again on the same claim in an F–1 court, and if F–1's application of that rule in this case would pass constitutional muster,[7] F–2 has an obligation under federal law to apply that rule whether or not its own preclusion rule is to the contrary.[8]

This federal obligation has broad ramifications. First, and most important, it means that F–1's policy decisions about the appropriate scope of preclusion will almost always trump any contrary policy of F–2. If, for example, F–1 takes a transactional

that would otherwise be constitutionally entitled to such recognition?)

7. One example of a case in which the Constitution would stand in the way of preclusion: a plaintiff obtains a default judgment in F–1 against a defendant who made no appearance in the action and over whom there was no territorial jurisdiction. In such a case, F–2 would not be obligated to recognize (or to enforce) the judgment over the defendant's objection, and indeed, would be constitutionally precluded from doing so. *See, e.g.,* York v. Texas, 137 U.S. 15, 21 (1890).

8. *See* RESTATEMENT (SECOND) OF CONFLICT OF LAWS §§ 93–97, 106, 117 (1971 and 1988 rev.), and authorities cited in the Reporter's Notes to those sections. As stated in §§ 106 and 117, this obligation exists even if the judgment of F–1 was based on an error of fact or law (§ 106), or was in conflict with the strong public policy of F–2 (§ 117).

This obligation with respect to civil judgments of sister states should be contrasted with the rules in the criminal sphere. A single act or course of conduct may violate the criminal laws of more than one jurisdiction, and a conviction or acquittal with respect to that act or course of conduct in F–1 does not constitutionally preclude a subsequent criminal prosecution for a comparable offense under the laws of F–2. *See, e.g.,* Bartkus v. Illinois, 359 U.S. 121 (1959) (federal prosecution followed by state prosecution); Heath v. Alabama, 474 U.S. 82 (1985) (prosecution in one state followed by prosecution in another state). The contrast, however, is not an irrational one: in the criminal context, one jurisdiction lacks the authority to prosecute for violation of the laws of another jurisdiction.

view of the scope of a claim while F–2 takes a far narrower view, F–1's view must be honored by F–2, as it must honor the views of F–1 on the kinds of judgments that will operate as a bar. And even if F–1 departs from the general view that issue preclusive effect may be given only to issues actually litigated, and, say, accords such effect to matters stipulated or admitted, F–2 must similarly honor that departure. Finally, an error of substantive law that contributed to the judgment in F–1 may not serve as the basis for denying preclusive effect, even if the error turns out to be a mistaken application of the law of F–2.[9]

This state of the law raises two questions. First, is it sound: Were we starting from scratch, would we decide that it is wise to tie the hands of F–2 in this way? And second, if the limitation on F–2's freedom to apply its own preclusion rules in such a case is wise as a general matter, are there situations in which a departure from that obligation is warranted?

9. *See, e.g.,* Fauntleroy v. Lum, 210 U.S. 230 (1908). The action in *Fauntleroy* was one brought in a Mississippi court to enforce a Missouri judgment for damages. The Supreme Court, applying the Full Faith and Credit Clause, held that enforcement could not be denied on the ground that Missouri's application of Mississippi law in rendering the initial judgment violated Mississippi's public policy. *A fortiori*, the Missouri judgment would have been constitutionally entitled to *recognition* in a Mississippi court.

Of course, in such a case, Missouri may allow its own courts to grant relief from the judgment under a rule comparable to FED. R. CIV. P. 60(b), but it is not constitutionally required to do so.

My response to the first of these questions is yes. An integral part of our understanding of the judicial process is that a judgment rendered by a court is entitled to respect, and within constitutional limits, the proper scope of that respect should be determined by the law of the forum that rendered the judgment. After all, if the preclusive effect of an F–1 judgment were a matter within the broad discretion of F–2, that effect could not even be known with certainty until the litigants knew the identity of F–2, and even then the respect to be accorded F–2's judgments in F–3 would be a matter of similar speculation–and so on. The authority of F–1 would be undermined, as would the reasonable expectations of the litigants. As one commentator has astutely argued, the preclusion law of a jurisdiction is essentially litigation-oriented, *i.e.*, most preclusion rules are "trans-substantive" and are designed to aid the parties and the courts in predicting the consequences of a judgment and thus in determining the proper level of investment in (or value of) a settlement.[10] Small wonder, then, that one American statesman (I'm not sure who) observed that the Full Faith and Credit Clause is one of the strong constitutional bonds holding the Nation together.

But the second question—possible limits on the scope of this principle—remains, and has perturbed courts and commentators for generations. The question may itself be subdivided: (a) What instances, if

10. The point is forcefully made and developed in Howard M. Erichson, *Interjurisdictional Preclusion*, 96 MICH. L. REV. 945 (1998).

any, warrant a decision by F–2 denying an F–1 judgment the preclusive effect that F–1 would give it? (b) What instances, if any, warrant a decision by F–2 giving an F–1 judgment *more* preclusive effect than F–1 would give it?

As a matter of statutory interpretation, both aspects of the question may be settled by the requirement of § 1738 that F–1's judgment receive *the same* full faith and credit that F–1 would give it. Perhaps the discussion should end there, and indeed the instances are rare in which F–2 would be likely to consider (or to get away with) giving *less* preclusive effect to an F–1 judgment that F–1 would (and constitutionally could) give it. An apparent exception—one that has not been beyond criticism—involves a case in which F–1 dismisses the action because its own statute of limitations has run. If the same claim is then brought against the same defendant in F–2, F–2 may decide (because of its own "borrowing" statute or for other reasons) to hold the claim barred in F–2. But under present law, at least if F–1's dismissal is not clearly designed to bar any and all future assertions of the claim, F–2 is not constitutionally required to impose a bar if it has a longer statute that has not yet run.[11] The rationale is apparently that a dismissal

11. *See* RESTATEMENT (SECOND) OF CONFLICT OF LAWS § 110, cmt. b (1971); RSJ § 19, cmt. f. In the Reporter's Note to RSJ § 19, the general rule of non-preclusion in this situation is criticized, and some contrary decisions noted. In the 1988 revision of the Conflicts Restatement, § 110, comment b was rewritten to indicate that F–2 may choose not to apply its own statute of limitations in this situation, and in the same revision § 142 was

on statute of limitations grounds is akin to a dismissal for lack of territorial jurisdiction or for forum non conveniens; since statutes of limitations are designed to implement a policy of protecting F–1's courts from litigating stale claims, there is no basis for closing the doors of F–2 if F–2's own policies tolerate a longer period for the commencement of an action. But the difficulty is that statutes of limitations are not simply written to protect courts; they are designed to give repose to those who may be accused of wrongdoing. And the time available for suit involves a balance between the need for such repose and the gravity and nature of the alleged wrong. Moreover, it is troubling that a plaintiff can have several bites at the apple: if F–1's law provides that the defendant is entitled to repose, try F–2; it may be friendlier to the plaintiff.[12]

Are there other instances in which F–2 may constitutionally give less preclusive effect to an F–1 judgment than F–1 can and does constitutionally give? One such instance may be found in the area of injunctive decrees. Just as the nature and extent of

rewritten to indicate those situations in which application of F–2's own limitations period would be inappropriate. For a full discussion devoted to the many difficult issues raised by the statute of limitations in the context of interstate conflicts of laws, including an analysis of the 1988 revision of § 142 (discussed above), see RUSSELL J. WEINTRAUB, COMMENTARY ON THE CONFLICT OF LAWS § 3.2C2 (4th ed. 2000).

12. Interestingly, if F–1 has a borrowing statute that refers it to the limitations period of F–2, and F–1 dismisses on the ground that F–2's limitations period has run, F–2 is surely bound to give that determination issue preclusive (if not claim preclusive) effect, even if F–1 made a serious error in applying F–2's law.

the enforceability of an F–1 injunctive decree in F–2 is uncertain (*supra* p. 120), so the claim preclusive effect of such a judgment is not fully resolved. If the plaintiff's action for injunctive relief in F–1 is denied on grounds that operate as a bar in F–1, plaintiff will also be barred in F–2 (RSJ § 18 cmt. d). But if a plaintiff obtains equitable relief in F–1 and cannot "enforce" the judgment in F–2,[13] it would be ironic to conclude that the plaintiff's claim is at the same time merged in the judgment so that a new action on the same claim cannot be brought in F–2. (And if it can, plaintiff can doubtless claim the benefit of issue preclusion with respect to issues actually litigated and necessary to F–1's judgment.)

Another area in which there is some support in both case and commentary for allowing F–2 to give less preclusive effect than would F–1 lies in the

13. Difficult questions arise with respect to the enforceability of an F–1 injunction in F–2. *See* authorities cited *supra* note 3. In Baker v. General Motors Corp., 522 U.S. 222 (1998), the Supreme Court held that a Michigan state court decree enjoining a former GM employee from testifying against the company in certain matters could not serve as the basis for preventing the employee from testifying in a federal court action brought against GM by a plaintiff who had not been a party to (or even on notice of) the Michigan proceeding. In the course of its opinion, the Court stated: "Enforcement measures do not travel with the sister state judgment as preclusive effects do; such measures remain subject to the even-handed control of forum law." *Id.* at 235. Thus, the *Baker* Court continued, "[o]rders commanding action or inaction have been denied enforcement in a sister State when they purported to accomplish an official act within the exclusive province of that other State or interfered with litigation over which the ordering State had no authority." *Id. See also* RESTATEMENT (SECOND) OF CONFLICT OF LAWS § 103, cmt. b (1971).

realm of nonmutual preclusion. As one commentator put it: "The major values served by nonmutual preclusion [at least in its broader manifestations] lie in the public costs of relitigation and the fear of inconsistency. A later court [in another jurisdiction] should be free to assume the costs of relitigation. And a first court should not be able to inflict on others its timorous fears of being proved wrong."[14] But the Supreme Court has not yet addressed this issue squarely, and the argument just quoted is far from conclusive. Not only is it difficult to reconcile with the relevant statutory and constitutional language but it fails to consider other policy considerations that may well have led F–1 to abandon its mutuality rule. For example, F–1 may take the view that if litigant A has been afforded every opportunity and incentive to litigate to the hilt and loses (knowing that he is litigating in a forum that has abandoned mutuality), it imposes an unfair burden on A's future adversaries to require them to litigate the same matter all over again. Is that policy consideration somehow diminished because the second litigation occurs in a different jurisdiction?[15]

14. 18 CHARLES A. WRIGHT, ARTHUR R. MILLER & EDWARD H. COOPER, FEDERAL PRACTICE AND PROCEDURE § 4465, at 617 (1981). *See also* authorities cited *id.* § 4465, at n. 69 (Supp. 2000).

15. Additional arguments against allowing F–2 to give less preclusive effect in this situation are advanced by Erichson, *supra* note 10, at 996. These arguments, which have a broader application to the choice between the preclusion law of F–1 and F–2, are discussed below, pp. 133–34.

One case worthy of note, and to some extent at odds with the argument in text, is Thomas v. Washington Gas Light Co., 448 U.S. 261 (1980), in which the Supreme Court allowed Thomas,

Even more uncertainty surrounds the question whether and to what extent F–2 may give F–1's judgment *greater* preclusive effect than F–1 would give it. Thus in the case of The Accident, consider the effect of a judgment *against* A in her F–1 suit against B. If F–1 adheres to the mutuality rule (*see supra* p. 102) but F–2 does not, may C invoke *issue preclusion* when sued by A in F–2? And if F–2, like New Jersey, has adopted the "entire controversy" rule (*see supra* p. 104), but F–1 has not, may C plead *claim preclusion* when sued by A in F–2? (If A lost the first action on a ground not relevant to her claim against C, claim preclusion would clearly be more useful to C in the second action.)

Again, the statutory requirement that "the same" faith and credit be accorded may end the discussion; surely "more" is not "the same." But perhaps in context, the phrase was used to make certain that a judgment was given at least as much credit as in F–1. If so, there may be room enough in

after settling an administrative claim for workers compensation in Virginia, to pursue a claim for the same injury in (and under the law of) the District of Columbia. The Court noted that Thomas could have sought an award in either jurisdiction (since Thomas resided and was hired in D.C. and the injury occurred in Virginia) and that there were "critical differences between a court of general jurisdiction and an administrative agency with limited statutory authority." *Id.* at 281–82. In particular, the Virginia Commission "could and did establish the full measure of [Thomas's] rights under Virginia law, but it neither could nor purported to determine his rights under the law of the District of Columbia." *Id.* at 282. Thus the key to the holding appeared to rest on the difference between the limited authority of an agency and the general jurisdiction of a civil court (which includes the authority to apply the law of other jurisdictions).

the statute to accommodate the special interests of
F–2, as long as they do not undermine any legiti-
mate concerns of F–1.

There is Supreme Court precedent indicating that
a state may not give the judgment of another state
"greater efficacy" than the rendering state would
give it.[16] But more recent lower court decisions
speak with less clarity, and even point in a contrary
direction.[17] And academic kibitzers have expressed a
range of opinions.[18] Under one view, F–2 should be
free to follow its own rule, at least if the greater
effect is foreseeable in the sense that the party to be
precluded should have foreseen the possibility

16. *E.g.,* Board of Public Works v. Columbia College, 84 U.S.
(17 Wall.) 521, 529 (1873); *see also* Migra v. Warren City School
Dist., 465 U.S. 75, 88 (1984) (White, J., concurring).

17. Thus, New Jersey applied its former "entire controversy"
rule, *see supra* pp. 104–05 (under which a non-party to a prior
action could obtain the benefits of claim preclusion), to allow a
defense of claim preclusion by a non-party to a prior action
partially litigated in *another* state, even though that state did not
adhere to the rule and would have rejected the defense. *See*
Mortgageling Corp. v. Commonwealth Land Title Ins. Co., 662
A.2d 536 (N.J.1995). *Cf.* Hart v. American Airlines, Inc., 304
N.Y.S.2d 810 (Sup.Ct.1969) (giving the judgment of a Texas
federal court in a diversity case more preclusive effect than a
Texas state court would have given it). The federal-state issues
involved (but not recognized) in the *Hart* case are discussed in
Section C, *infra.*

18. *See, e.g.,* 18 WRIGHT ET AL., *supra* note 14, §§ 4465, 4467;
id. (2000 Supp.); Erichson, *supra* note 10, at 994; Graham C.
Lilly, *The Symmetry of Preclusion,* 54 OHIO ST. L.J. 289, 328
(1993); *Cf.* Gene R. Shreve, *Preclusion and Federal Choice of
Law,* 64 TEX. L. REV. 1209, 1252–57 (1986).

The Erichson article cited above is especially useful because it
contains a valuable survey of those areas where jurisdictions
disagree on important questions of preclusion doctrine.

(probability?) of an action in F–2, and if F–1's interests in finality are not undercut (and they seldom would be by giving a judgment added effect). After all, F–2's rule favoring preclusion is designed at least in part to ease the burden on its own courts, and those who litigate in them. Under a competing view, greater preclusive effect should not be given by F–2, except perhaps in a case in which the more expansive preclusion rule is linked to a specific substantive right and the law of F–1 is not the source of that right.[19] After all, F–1 has a substantial interest in limiting the effects of its judgments in other forums, since its own policies toward litigation (*e.g.*, the extent of the parties' expenditures of time and effort) may well be affected by the preclusive effect to be given to the judgment in the initial action. Moreover, it would be ironic if, say, a judgment that F–1 would not give claim preclusive effect were given such an effect in F–2, thus requiring F–1 to give it that effect if the claim were later to be pursued there.[20] Finally,

19. One possible example of a preclusion rule linked to a specific substantive right: the Kansas rule (discussed in Erichson, *supra* note 10, at 981–82, 1003) that limits the assertion of a claim preclusion defense by a non-party to a prior action to cases in which the prior action involved a question of comparative negligence.

20. If two inconsistent judgments are rendered in a single jurisdiction, the later of the two is the one entitled to preclusive effect. *See* RSJ § 15. The Supreme Court, in interpreting the constitutional obligation of Full Faith and Credit, has made this rule applicable to sister state judgments—even when the losing party in the second action tried without success to invoke the rules of preclusion in that action. Treinies v. Sunshine Mining Co., 308 U.S. 66 (1939).

under an intermediate view, F–2 may invoke its more expansive preclusion rule in the interest of freeing its own courts of the burden of relitigation– so long as the door-closing effect is limited to the courts of F–2, and does not prevent or limit suit in F–1, or F-*n*.[21]

The problem arises not only when F–1 and F–2 are both state courts, but when F–1 is state and F–2 is federal, and vice versa. (The latter two areas are discussed in the following sections of this chapter, but it should be noted here that in the last of the three situations, neither Article IV of the Constitution nor § 1738 is explicitly applicable.) My own view is that a general, if not an absolute, prohibition on giving more preclusive effect is the soundest resolution of a thorny problem. In the state-state situation, this result is supported not only by the text of the full faith and credit statute but by an important policy consideration.[22] When parties litigate in F–1, the degree of their investment and effort in the case—as well as their willingness to settle—is likely to be governed not only by the significance of the case itself but also by the preclusive effects of any disposition. And in predicting those effects, they are likely to look to the preclusion rules of the forum they are in. Indeed, were they "required" (*i.e.*, prodded by the possibility of greater preclusion somewhere else) to take the rules

21. *See* 18 WRIGHT ET AL., *supra* note 14, § 4467, at 645 (in the context of claim preclusion).

22. For a thorough and persuasive presentation of the policy argument, see Erichson, *supra* note 10, at 961–63.

of other forums into account, not only would the task of prediction become far harder, but F–1's policies underlying its own choice of preclusion rules might well be undermined. For example, as suggested above, a narrow approach by F–1 to a particular preclusion problem (like the definition of a "claim") might be based on the forum's desire to avoid overlitigation of a case, as well as the taking of appeals designed solely to ward off preclusive consequences in later cases.[23]

(One reader of this manuscript in draft, who disagrees with this conclusion, argues forcefully that if F–2 gives greater recognition to a judgment than F–1 would give, that action does not significantly undercut F–1's primary interest in protecting the finality of its judgments. Thus, he continues, F–2's decision to accord greater claim or issue preclusive effect to F–1's judgment is surely not prohibited by the Full Faith and Credit Clause. He concludes, again with considerable force, that the result advocated here, if defensible at all, should be grounded not in the Constitution itself but only in a statutory text (*e.g.,* use of the word "same" in § 1738 or in a rule of federal common law.)

The middle ground—F–2 closes its doors but nobody else's—does have a theoretical appeal. But as its advocates have recognized, it makes sense only

---

23. Moreover, as Erichson points out, the *potential* preclusive effect of a judgment is a matter of concern in every litigation (*i.e.,* every case filed in any F–1), but the *actual* preclusive effect of a prior judgment arises only in a relatively small fraction of cases—those in which a subsequent litigation in fact occurs outside F–1. *See id.* at 999–1001.

when the question is the "door-closing" one of claim preclusion, not when the court is asked to foreclose litigation of an *issue* in a case properly before it. And even in the claim preclusion context, what if, for reasons of territorial jurisdiction or, perhaps, choice of law, F–2 is the only available or practicable forum for the bringing of a second action? Moreover, as a practical matter, how likely is the court in F–2, in dismissing a case, to make clear to future courts that its dismissal is without prejudice to the commencement of an action in another jurisdiction? (If it doesn't, the default rule—that the extent of preclusion is determined by the preclusion rules of the last court to deal with the matter—may foreclose litigation of the claim in any other forum.[24])

B.   When F–1 Is a State Tribunal and F–2 Is a Federal Tribunal

---

If F–1 is a state *court* (as opposed to an adjudicative tribunal other than a court), and F–2 is a federal court, Congress has provided in § 1738 (by imposing the full faith and credit obligation on "every court within the United States ... ") that the preclusive effect of the judgment shall be the same as the effect the rendering court would give. Thus Congress has exercised a power it undoubtedly has—to impose on the federal courts a full faith and credit obligation in such cases that is essentially equivalent to the *constitutional* and statutory

24.   *See supra* note 20.

obligation imposed on the states.[25] As a result, much of the discussion in Section A of this chapter is fully applicable here.[26]

But the text of the statute does not refer in terms to the "internal" preclusion law of F–1; rather it

25. A related doctrine, based on the Supreme Court decisions in Rooker v. Fidelity Trust Co., 263 U.S. 413 (1923), and District of Columbia Court of Appeals v. Feldman, 460 U.S. 462 (1983), is not dealt with in text. Under the rationale of the *"Rooker-Feldman"* doctrine, a lower federal court may not sit in review of a state court decision (by entertaining a collateral attack, for example) because the reviewing function is reserved to the Supreme Court by the statutory provisions governing such review. (The doctrine does not in itself affect the role of the lower federal courts in entertaining habeas corpus petitions by state prisoners.) The *Rooker-Feldman* doctrine has its defenders, but it has been much criticized, largely on the ground that if it adds to the existing restraints on federal courts imposed by the rules of interjurisdictional preclusion (including 28 U.S.C. § 1738), any such addition is unnecessary and undesirable. *See, e.g.,* RICHARD H. FALLON, DANIEL J. MELTZER & DAVID L. SHAPIRO, HART & WECHSLER'S THE FEDERAL COURTS AND THE FEDERAL SYSTEM 1501–04, and authorities cited (4th ed. 1996) (hereafter cited as HART & WECHSLER), and authorities cited, *id.* at 216–17 (2000 Supp.).

Although the Supreme Court has applied this doctrine only twice, once in the *Rooker* case and once in the *Feldman* case, it has been given a generous reception in the lower federal courts, and some circuits (but not all) have even applied it to bar a federal court action by a non-party to the state proceeding (whether or not such an action would be barred by the rules of preclusion). *See, e.g.,* Lemonds v. St. Louis County, 222 F.3d 488 (8th Cir.2000), *cert. denied sub nom.* Halbman v. St. Louis County, 121 S.Ct. 1168 (2001).

26. For examples of cases in which the Supreme Court has held that, in determining the preclusive effects of a prior state court judgment, federal courts must follow the preclusion rules of that state, see Allen v. McCurry, 449 U.S. 90 (1980); Kremer v. Chemical Constr. Co., 456 U.S. 461 (1982); Migra v. Warren City

requires that a state court's judgment be given the same faith and credit as it has "by law or usage in the courts of such State.... " Thus, it is possible that, as a matter of federal law, operating on the states through the Supremacy Clause, a state would be obligated to follow federal preclusion law with respect to one of its own judgments. Surely, for example, Congress could provide that when a federal claim or issue is adjudicated in a state court, federal law (*i.e.*, federal common law or a particular statutory preclusion rule) shall govern the preclusive effect of the judgment in a subsequent action. In such a case, one might conclude not that § 1738 had been superseded but rather that the preclusion rule to be applied in accordance with that provision is federal.[27]

This possibility exists in theory, but the Supreme Court—clearly aware that the states have an important interest in the extent to which preclusive effect will be accorded to their judgments—has never squarely imposed such a federal preclusion rule directly on the states. Instead, it has consistently indicated that the preclusion law of the state that rendered the judgment will (at least presumptively) furnish the rule to be followed in the subsequent

School Dist., 465 U.S. 75 (1984); Parsons Steel, Inc. v. First Alabama Bank, 474 U.S. 518 (1986).

27. For full development of this point (and of related arguments), see Stephen B. Burbank, *Interjurisdictional Preclusion, Full Faith and Credit and Federal Common Law: A General Approach,* 71 CORNELL L. REV. 733 (1986).

federal action.[28]

Because the obligation imposed on the federal courts is statutory and not constitutional, there also exists the possibility of an express or implicit exception to this obligation. Indeed the question whether to recognize such an exception to § 1738 is a close relative of the question, just discussed, of whether § 1738 itself ever permits federal preclusion law to displace state law with respect to the effect of a state court judgment.

Even in cases in which a reasonable basis exists for finding an exception, the Supreme Court has in general insisted that the relevant preclusion rule is that of the state that rendered the initial judgment. Thus, in the face of a strong argument that the distrust of state institutions underlying 42 U.S.C. § 1983[29] warrants an exception to the demands of § 1738, the Court has held that state preclusion law governs on matters of both claim and issue preclusion when the subsequent action is brought under § 1983.[30] And in a concurring opinion in one of these cases, three Justices noted some ancient authority that precludes a federal court from giving

28. *See* authorities cited *supra* note 26. In one case, Haring v. Prosise, 462 U.S. 306, 317–23 (1983), the Court first decided that a state court decision had no preclusive effect under state law and then rejected an argument that "this Court should create a special rule of preclusion which nevertheless would bar litigation" of a subsequent action on a federal claim in a federal court. *Id.* at 317.

29. A widely-used civil rights statute—originally enacted in 1871—that provides a private remedy for violations of federal rights committed under color of state law.

30. *See* Kremer v. Chemical Constr. Corp., 456 U.S. 461 (1982); Migra v. Warren City School Dist., 465 U.S. 75 (1984).

state judgments *greater* preclusive effect than the rendering state would give.[31]

What of the situation in which, after a judgment is rendered in a state court, a second action that is brought in a federal court falls within the *exclusive* subject matter jurisdiction of the federal courts? Does § 1738 require that the federal court give the state judgment the same preclusive effect that the rendering state would give? The question is a strange one, since by definition the rendering state would have no subject matter jurisdiction over the second action. Yet, the long arm of state preclusion law has been held to reach such cases. First, the Court has held, in *Matsushita Electric Industrial v. Epstein,*[32] that if the state court action is settled, and the settlement covers *all* claims arising out of the matter in suit (even those within exclusive federal jurisdiction), the effect of the settlement is to bar the assertion of a covered federal claim in a federal court. And in a class action that meets the prerequisites for binding absent class members, the claim preclusive effect will extend to everyone in the class.[33] Given the state court's lack of authority to adjudicate the federal claims in such a case, the *Matsushita* decision is difficult to reconcile with accepted preclusion doctrine and can perhaps best be explained in terms of the ability of contracting parties (*i.e.*, the parties to the settlement) to bind

31. *See* Migra v. Warren City School Dist., 465 U.S. 75, 88, and cases cited (1984) (White, J., concurring, in an opinion joined by Burger, C.J. and Powell, J.).

32. 516 U.S. 367, 385–86 (1996).

33. *Id..* at 378–79.

themselves and others they represent. But the Court's emphasis was on the claim-preclusive effect of the judgment.

Second, the Court has held, in the *Marrese* case,[34] that if a state judgment on a state claim is followed by a federal court action between the same parties on a closely related claim falling within exclusive federal jurisdiction, the first duty of the federal court is to refer to state law to determine the preclusive effect of the state judgment. "Only if state law indicates that a particular claim or issue would be barred, is it necessary to determine if an exception to § 1738 should apply."[35] The *Marrese* case is interesting from several perspectives: It underscores the critical role of state preclusion law in such cases. It insists that state law must be consulted even when—given the exclusivity of federal court jurisdiction—the second action could not be brought in a state court (but the state may have an analogous precedent which, like RSJ § 26, would not apply claim preclusion under similar circumstances). And it does suggest the possibility of an implied exception to the rule of § 1738 when application of the rule would pose a serious threat to the effectuation of federal policy.

Third, since the existence of exclusive federal jurisdiction over particular claims does not preclude a state court from adjudicating issues that may be critical to the determination of those claims, daunt-

34. Marrese v. American Acad. of Orthopaedic Surgeons, 470 U.S. 373 (1985).

35. *Id.* at 386.

ing questions of the proper scope of issue preclusion may arise when the second action is brought in a federal court. Take three examples:

(1) In a state court contract action brought by A against B for failure to pay royalties under a patent license agreement, it is determined that the agreement did not go into effect until a certain date, and that royalties may therefore be collected after but not before that date. What is the issue preclusive effect of that determination in a subsequent federal court action for patent infringement brought by A against B?

(2) In a similar state court action by A against B, the defense that A's patent is invalid is sustained. What is the issue preclusive effect of this determination in a subsequent federal court action for patent infringement brought by A against B?

(3) Same state court action as in case (2) If the state has abandoned the mutuality doctrine, what is the issue preclusive effect of the state court's determination that A's patent is invalid in a later federal court patent infringement action brought by A against C?

A reasonable argument could be made that issue preclusion is available in all three cases. But surely, the first case, involving a determination of fact well within the state court's competence, is the strongest candidate for preclusion. The second, involving a question that the exclusive jurisdiction provision was undoubtedly designed to assign—primarily if not exclusively—to the federal courts for decision, is a good deal weaker.[36] And the third seems the weakest of all, since allowing NMIP[37] in such a case would give the state courts authority (subject only to Supreme Court review on certiorari) to declare a patent invalid as against the entire world. Perhaps the optimal resolution is to deprive the state courts of jurisdiction altogether by requiring removal to federal court when a defense of patent invalidity is raised. An even more innovative step would be to permit a direct appeal of the federal patent issue from the highest available state court to a specialized federal appellate court (the Federal Circuit). But in the absence of such changes, the best approach to the scope of issue preclusion in cases like those in the examples above may be one calling for close examination on a case-by-case basis of the appropriateness of according preclusive effect to a particular state court finding. There is authority to support such an approach.[38]

36. Indeed, Congress has gone further in an effort to ensure the existence of both experience and expertise in patent (and certain related) cases, conferring on the Court of Appeals for the Federal Circuit exclusive appellate jurisdiction over appeals from *any* federal district court in any case in which the district court's jurisdiction was based "in whole or in part, on section 1338 [of Title 28—the provision for exclusive federal district court jurisdiction in such cases]." 28 U.S.C. § 1295(a)(1).

37. For an explanation of this and related acronyms, see *supra* p. 106.

38. *Compare, e.g.,* Lyons v. Westinghouse Elec. Corp., 222 F.2d 184, 189 (2d Cir.1955) (holding that a state court's determination of an antitrust defense did not bind a federal court in a subsequent antitrust action) (L. Hand, J.), *with, e.g.,* Vanderveer v. Erie Malleable Iron Co., 238 F.2d 510, 513 (3d Cir.1956) (according issue preclusive effect, in a federal patent infringe-

In some instances, the notion that subject matter jurisdiction is subject to collateral attack—a notion that, as we have seen, is subject to significant limitations when the second action is brought in the same jurisdiction (*see supra* pp. 25–29)—has been used to vindicate federal authority over a particular controversy. In one case, *United States v. United States Fidelity & Guaranty Co.*,[39] the Court held that the United States and the Indian Nations under its protection were immune from suit in a state court, that the immunity could not be waived by failure to assert it, and that a state court judgment against the defendants in a prior state court action was therefore open to collateral attack. And in *Kalb v. Feuerstein*,[40] a state court judgment and subsequent foreclosure sale of mortgaged property, all of which occurred while a petition was pending in federal court under the Bankruptcy Act, were held void in a later federal court proceeding by the mortgagors.

Finally, on more than one occasion the Supreme Court has indicated that if a state court decides a federal question in a case that is not subject to federal review (because, for example, the state proceeding does not satisfy Article III's requirement of a justiciable case or controversy), then the state court judgment may be denied preclusive effect.[41]

ment action, to a state court's prior determination that a patent did not cover certain goods). For a general discussion of this problem, see RSJ § 86.

39.   309 U.S. 506 (1940).

40.   308 U.S. 433 (1940).

41.   *See, e.g.,* ASARCO Inc. v. Kadish, 490 U.S. 605 (1989) (dictum); Fidelity Nat. Bank & Trust Co. v. Swope, 274 U.S. 123

In sum, the special relationship between the state and federal systems and between state and federal law, and the non-constitutional character of the mandate of § 1738, ensure that the resolution of the preclusion problems discussed in this section will often be difficult. But a strong presumption that the mandate of § 1738 will be applied would serve not only to implement congressional purpose in enacting the statute but to enhance predictability and buttress the policy choices made by the states in selecting a preclusion rule.

C.   When F–1 Is a Federal Tribunal

1.   *And F–2 is a State Tribunal.* Return with me once again to the case of The Accident. Assume that after A sues B in a federal court, judgment is rendered for B. A then sues C in a state court for the same injuries resulting from the same accident.

One point at the outset: although some early decisions pointed in a different direction, it is now recognized that the preclusive effect of the federal court judgment in such a case is not directly governed by the text of either the Constitution or the

(1927) (dictum). Also, as noted above, p. 7, the statutory provisions governing the availability of the writ of federal habeas corpus for state prisoners have been consistently understood to override general rules of preclusion as they affect state court determinations. However, recent changes in the federal laws governing this writ have been interpreted to require greater deference to state court determinations that are challenged in federal habeas proceedings. *See* Williams v. Taylor, 529 U.S. 362 (2000).

provisions of § 1738.[42] At the same time, there is no doubt that the federal judicial power over cases and controversies entails the power to render a judgment with binding effect—binding both in terms of its enforceability and its recognition not just in other federal courts but in other American jurisdictions. Thus, in the absence of any act of Congress governing the effect of a particular judgment—and such legislation is rare—the rules of preclusion are, to a significant extent, determined by federal common law.[43] And this federal common law, like federal statutory and constitutional law, is binding on the states through the Supremacy Clause.

Assume then—though it is hard to imagine how—that A's initial federal court suit against B was founded on federal question jurisdiction. Courts and commentators agree—surely with good reason—that federal law (ordinarily but not always federal common law) controls the preclusive effect of the judgment in subsequent litigation, whether F–2 is a federal or a state court. Thus, if all the prerequisites to NMOIP articulated by the Supreme Court in the *Parklane* decision are met (*supra* p. 109–10), C should be able to invoke issue preclusion in a subsequent action against A in a state as well as in a federal court. And if B later sues A in a state

42. *See* Semtek Int'l, Inc. v. Lockheed Martin Corp., 121 S.Ct. 1021 (2001).

43. *See id.* The relation between the federal common law rules of preclusion, the preclusion rules of the forum state, and the provisions of the Federal Rules of Civil Procedure (for example, Rules 13(a) and 41) is a major aspect of the remaining discussion in this section.

court for damages arising out of the same transaction, B's failure to assert his claim as a counterclaim in the first action should bar its later assertion, in light of the "compulsory counterclaim" provision in Federal Rule 13(a).[44] Finally, if the action by A was dismissed on certain threshold grounds—for example, a failure to prosecute, or a failure to comply with a discovery order, or the running of the statute of limitations—the claim preclusive effect of that judgment if A sues B again in a state court should be determined by looking to what a federal court would do if it were F–2. The law that determines the preclusive effect of such a judgment, in other words, is purely and simply federal.[45]

44. The question of the extent to which a Federal Rule of Civil Procedure can, consistently with the Rules Enabling Act (28 U.S.C. § 2072), control the preclusive effect of a federal judgment is one that remains unresolved. For the view that it cannot, see Burbank, *supra* note 27, at 772–75. But as Burbank concedes, and as others have agreed, the Federal Rules can at the least create a context that will, and should, affect the content of the federal common law rule. *See id.* at 775; Erichson, *supra* note 10, at 1006 & n. 307.

45. Even so, the content of the federal preclusion rule in the particular context remains to be determined. For example, the federal rule (which is not directly controlled by the Full Faith and Credit Clause or § 1738) may allow a state court, in a subsequent proceeding, to give a federal judgment greater preclusive effect than the federal court would give it. (But for reasons stated above, pp. 133–34, such a result seems undesirable.) Alternatively, the federal rule may permit a state court to give a federal judgment less preclusive effect (as to determinations of issues of state law, for example) than might be required by the Full Faith and Credit Clause or § 1738. *See generally* David L. Shapiro, *State Courts and Federal Declaratory Judgments,* 74 Nw. U. L. Rev. 759 (1979).

But change the case so that jurisdiction in the first action is based on diversity of citizenship rather than a federal question (or so that the claim in question is for some other reason one for which state law supplies the rules of decision). Assume further that F–1 is in a state that has no compulsory counterclaim rule, that still honors the doctrine of mutuality, and that does not regard any decision as claim preclusive unless it is either settled or goes to judgment after trial of the merits. What law governs in a subsequent action in a state court with respect to the scope of claim or issue preclusion?

The problem turns out to be surprisingly difficult because of the interplay of pre-*Erie*[46] Supreme Court precedent, the factors militating in favor of a uniform federal body of preclusion law governing the binding effect of a federal judgment, and the significance of state law in diversity cases under both statute (the Rules of Decision Act), and precedent (*Erie* and its successors).[47] The problem is

46. Erie R.R. v. Tompkins, 304 U.S. 64 (1938).

47. The Rules of Decision Act, 28 U.S.C. § 1652, provides, in its present version, that unless otherwise required or provided by federal law, "[t]he laws of the several states ... shall be regarded as rules of decision in civil actions in the courts of the United States, in cases where they apply." And the *Erie* decision held, in a federal diversity case, that the requirement of that statute included the rules developed by the state courts in the exercise of their common law authority. (The Court also stated that this result was constitutionally mandated.) But as has frequently been noted, the Act and its interpretation in *Erie* are also relevant outside the diversity context, as in the case of a state law claim that arises under the supplemental jurisdiction statute (28 U.S.C. § 1367), or in a bankruptcy proceeding. *See, e.g.,* HART & WECHSLER, *supra* note 25, at 692, 767–68.

further complicated to the extent that the provisions of the Federal Rules of Civil Procedure appear to be relevant in the particular case.

As to pre-*Erie* Supreme Court precedent, an important decision is *Dupasseur v. Rochereau*,[48] which held in 1874 (on review of a state court decision) that the preclusive effect of a prior federal court judgment in a diversity case should be determined on the basis of the effect that would be given to an analogous judgment by the courts of the state in which the federal court was located. In the era following the *Erie* decision, a number of commentators addressed the problem, and proposed a variety of resolutions, but the Supreme Court did not speak to the question again until 2001, in *Semtek International, Inc. v. Lockheed Martin Corp.*[49] And in that case the Court, though holding that the *Dupasseur* decision was not controlling precedent, ended up adhering to the same approach.

In *Semtek,* the plaintiff (Semtek) had sued Lockheed on a state law claim in a California state court, and after Lockheed removed the case to a California federal court on the basis of diversity of citizenship, the action was dismissed "on the merits and with prejudice" on the ground that the action was barred by California's statute of limitations. Following the dismissal, Semtek filed a second action against Lockheed, based on the same claim, in a Maryland state court. The Maryland courts dismissed the action on grounds of claim preclusion, holding that

48. 88 U.S. 130 (1874).

49. 121 S.Ct. 1021 (2001).

whether or not the California courts would have given the prior dismissal claim preclusive effect, and even though Maryland law itself permitted the second action to be brought because its own statute of limitations had not yet run, the dismissal was required by federal law, and particularly by Rule 41(b) of the Federal Rules of Civil Procedure, the relevant text of which is set out in the margin.[50]

In an opinion reversing the judgment below, Justice Scalia, writing for a unanimous Court, first determined that *Dupasseur* was not controlling because the result in that case may have been influenced by the since-repealed Conformity Act, which required federal courts to adhere to the procedural rules of the forum state. The Court then turned to the difficult question of the effect of Rule 41(b), and concluded that the term "upon the merits" in the rule did not require that the judgment in question be given claim preclusive effect but *only* that, unlike a dismissal without prejudice, a Rule 41(b) dismissal on the merits meant simply that the action could not again be filed in the same court. (This somewhat strained interpretation was expressly influenced by the Court's concern that to give the provision broader effect would raise serious questions under both the Rules Enabling Act[51] and the *Erie*

50. That rule states that, "[u]nless the court ... otherwise specifies," and with certain exceptions not relevant in the *Semtek* case, an involuntary dismissal "operates as an adjudication upon the merits."

51. *See supra* note 44. That Act prohibits the promulgation of any rule that would "abridge, enlarge or modify any substantive right."

doctrine.) In the absence of any controlling constitutional provision, statute, or procedural rule, the matter was governed by "federal common law." The Court concluded that in a diversity case, in which the controlling substantive law is that of the forum state, the preclusive effect of the federal court's judgment should normally also be determined by the law of that state. But, the Court cautioned, "[t]his federal [common law] reference to state law will not obtain ... in situations in which the state law is not compatible with federal interests. If, for example, state law did not accord claim preclusive effect to dismissals for willful violation of discovery orders, federal courts' interest in the integrity of their own processes might justify a contrary federal rule."[52]

The Court's opinion in *Semtek* threaded its way through a difficult and complex maze of interrelated issues: issues of interpretation of the rules of procedure and deeper issues of the proper—and even constitutionally mandated—relationship between state and federal law. Doubtless, the decision will prove controversial in both its result and its rationale, particularly with respect to its effect on earlier precedents involving the relationship between the Federal Rules of Civil Procedure and the *Erie* doctrine. But the opinion did resolve some long-debated questions about the preclusive effects of a federal court judgment in cases in which state law supplies the rules of decision. There will, of course, be many questions that are bound to follow in its wake. For

52.   121 S.Ct. at 1028–29.

example, what kinds of federal interests might warrant a federal rule of preclusion that overrides normally applicable state law in determining the effects of a judgment in a diversity case (or in other federal court litigation—such as the adjudication of a claim by or against a bankrupt—that is governed by state law)? And what is the significance of other federal procedural rules, such as the compulsory counterclaim provision in Rule 13(a) or the class action provisions of Rule 23? Although such questions remain open, a framework for resolving them has been established.

2. *And F–2 Is Another Federal Tribunal.* If F–1 and F–2 are both federal courts, and the F–1 action was one governed by federal substantive law, it seems clear that the questions of preclusion are the same as those dealt with in Chapters II and III. In other words, the "federal" entity in this context is analogous to a "state," and the rules of preclusion will be those developed as a matter of federal statutory law (including any applicable rules of procedure) and federal common law for the governance of federal business. And indeed, many Supreme Court decisions have reflected the Court's recognition that in such cases, the governing rules of preclusion are shaped without regard to the particular rules of any state.[53]

But if the federal court in F–1 was adjudicating a case governed by state substantive law—a diversity

53. *See, e.g.,* Parklane Hosiery Co. v. Shore, 439 U.S. 322 (1979); Federated Dep't Stores, Inc. v. Moitie, 452 U.S. 394 (1981).

case, for example—the question is clearly affected by the Court's decision in the *Semtek* case. My own view of that effect depends in part on my assumption (a reasonable one, I believe) that the Court's interpretation of Rule 41(b) as referring only to the claim preclusive effect of a dismissal in the "same" court is a limitation of the provision to the very court that dismissed the action. On that assumption, it would appear that the preclusive effect of the F–1 judgment should be governed by the law of the state in which F–1 was located to the same extent that it would be if F–2 were a court of a sister state. Moreover, it should not matter whether the federal court's jurisdiction in F–2 is based on diversity or on the existence of a federal question.

There is, however, one caveat. The *Semtek* Court indicated that the reference to the law of the state in which F–1 was located might be overcome by a showing of incompatibility with federal interests. Those interests may be viewed as more compelling in some situations in which the second action is also brought in a federal court For example, suppose a federal court in a diversity case dismisses a complaint for failure to state a claim but gives the plaintiff leave to amend within 30 days—on the ground that a redrafted complaint might cure the defect in the original complaint. If the plaintiff ignores the opportunity to amend and some time later files a new action in a *state* court on the same claim (but drafts a better complaint), *Semtek*'s rationale may well allow the second action to proceed if the law of F–1's forum state would allow it. But if the second action is filed in another federal court, the federal interest in enforcing the time limits established by the original dismissal (as well as other factors) might lead to the conclusion that the permissive rule of the F–1 forum state should not be adhered to.

D. When F–1 Is a Tribunal of a Foreign Country and F–2 Is a Federal or State Tribunal in the United States

This final variation on the interjurisdictional theme is our first venture into the field of international law. The focus here will be on the case in which the initial judgment is rendered in another country and recognition is sought in an American (federal or state) tribunal.

Once again, important aspects of the problem may be illustrated by a variation on the hypothetical of The Accident, though it needs to be embellished a good bit. Suppose, then, that the original accident occurred in New Jersey, and that A was a citizen and resident of Fredonia (a small country in central Europe), while B and C were both citizens and residents of New Jersey. B and C, by a strange coincidence, are both geophysicists, and while they are attending an international geophysical conference in Fredonia, A (who has since returned home) brings suit against B in a Fredonian court for the personal injuries incurred in the accident. She does not include in her complaint any allegations relating to the damage to her car, nor does she join C as a defendant (because she is unaware of C's presence at the conference). B hires a lawyer to defend against the claim and loses (under standards of tort liability identical to New Jersey's). Judgment is entered for A for 20,000,000 zlotys (approximately $50,000).

We need to make some additional assumptions about the law of Fredonia. First, Fredonia's procedures meet all the standards of due process that would have to be met in the U.S. Second, Fredonia has a narrow doctrine of claim preclusion, under which the adjudication of a claim for personal injuries does not preclude a claim for property damage arising out of the same transaction. Third, Fredonia adheres to the rule of mutuality with respect to claim preclusion, and does not recognize the concept of issue preclusion at all. Finally, Fredonia has a law prohibiting its courts from recognizing or enforcing any foreign country judgment against one of its own citizens.[54]

54. Some of these assumptions are more realistic than others. For example, many countries do define a claim more narrowly than does the *Restatement*, and some countries do not recognize issue preclusion except in very limited situations. Moreover, insistence on reciprocity as a basis for recognition/enforcement is more common outside the U.S., and other countries have expressed concern over the recognized bases for territorial jurisdiction and the existence of "excessive" damage awards in U.S. courts. *See generally* Robert C. Casad, *Issue Preclusion and Foreign Country Judgments: Whose Law?*, 70 IOWA L. REV. 53 (1984); Linda J. Silberman & Andreas F. Lowenfeld, *A Different Challenge for the ALI: Herein of Foreign Country Judgments, an International Treaty, and an American Statute*, 75 IND. L.J. 635 (2000). *See also* Michael J. Waggoner, *Fifty Years of* Bernhard v.

B, who has no assets in Fredonia, returns to the U.S. at the end of the conference, and some months later, A brings an action against B and C in a New Jersey court. With respect to B, A seeks a New Jersey judgment enforcing her Fredonia judgment and also asserts a claim for property damage to her car. With respect to C, A asserts a claim for both her personal injuries and the damage to her car resulting from the accident.

We need to draw some base lines before considering how a New Jersey court should resolve the questions our case presents. First, nothing in any treaty, or in federal statutory or constitutional law *requires* New Jersey to give full faith and credit, or indeed any faith and credit, to such a judgment of a court of Fredonia or of any other foreign country.[55]

Bank of America *is Enough: Collateral Estoppel Should Require Mutuality But Res Judicata Should Not,* 12 Rev. Litig. 391 (1993): "[M]ost civil law countries do not have a rule against splitting a claim." *Id.* at 394 n.9. "Legal systems in France, Germany, Argentina, Japan, Sweden, and Mexico have only the most narrow use of collateral estoppel." *Id.* at 402 n.34.

55. There are a few specific federal statutes in this area, *e.g.*, 28 U.S.C. § 2467 (recently enacted), but they do not apply here, and generally do not apply. Nor is there any general international convention—applicable to the enforcement or recognition of the judgments of foreign courts—to which the U.S. is a party (of which more below).

In contrast, the United States is a party to the International Convention on the Recognition and Enforcement of Foreign Arbitral Awards (entered into force for the U.S. in 1970), 21 U.S.T. 2517. *See generally* Restatement (Third) of the Foreign Relations Law of the United States §§ 487–88 (1987) (hereafter cited as RTFRL). This Convention is binding on the states as well as on the national government, and thus questions of

Second, any *limitations* imposed by the federal Constitution on New Jersey's ability to grant enforcement or recognition to the Fredonia judgment would presumably be those arising from the Due Process Clause of the Fourteenth Amendment. If, for example, the Fredonia court had not acquired territorial jurisdiction over B under the standards established by the Supreme Court for the assertion of jurisdiction by a state or by the United States, or if B had not been given adequate notice of the Fredonia proceeding, B should have a constitutional objection to New Jersey's decision to enforce the judgment or give A the benefit of any rules of preclusion. Third, though this area (like many areas involving international choice of law) seems an especially appropriate one for the development of federal common law rules—rules that in this context would govern recognition and enforcement in both state and federal courts[56]—existing federal enforcement and recognition arising under the Convention are questions of federal law.

In addition, there has been considerable progress made in dealing with the special problems presented by the international aspects of child custody. These problems, and the efforts to deal with them through international agreement and domestic law, are fully discussed in a recent Symposium, *Celebrating Twenty Years: The Past and Promise of the 1980 Hague Convention on the Civil Aspects of International Child Abduction*, 33 N.Y.U. J. Int'l L. & Pol. 1–377 (2000).

56. *See, e.g.,* Casad, *supra* note 54, who states (at 79): "Although the Republic can survive without federalizing the law of foreign judgment recognition, the arguments in favor of that position are strong and the principal argument against it amounts to little more than inertia." Such a result could clearly be effectuated by a federal statute, but also appears to be within

precedent leaves it to the forum to decide whether and to what extent recognition and enforcement should be accorded.[57] It seems passing strange that the value to litigants of a foreign country judgment may vary from state to state, and indeed would doubtless mystify a Fredonian lawyer, but (to quote a famous character from an E.M. Forster novel) there it is.

Thus, as a matter of federal law, New Jersey has a good deal of freedom to grant or deny faith or credit to the Fredonian judgment. Reserving for later the effect of a Uniform Act (which has been adopted in original or modified form in many states, including New Jersey), and assuming for the moment that the state has enacted no relevant statute, a number of questions face the state court. In particular: (1) Should the court grant enforcement of the judgment against B? (2) Should the court apply its own concept of claim preclusion to bar a new action against B for property damage? (3) If not, should the court apply its own rules of issue preclusion to determine what issues of fact or law have been established as a result of the Fredonian judgment? (4) Should the court apply its own "entire controversy" rule (*see supra* p. 104) and allow C

the reach of federal common law. *Cf.* Banco Nacional de Cuba v. Sabbatino, 376 U.S. 398 (1964); Hart & Wechsler, *supra* note 25, at 806–810 (*Note on Sabbatino and the Federal Law of International Relations*).

57. Despite hints to the contrary in Hilton v. Guyot, 159 U.S. 113 (1895), the Court determined in Aetna Life Ins. Co. v. Tremblay, 223 U.S. 185 (1912), that a state court decision denying recognition to a Canadian judgment was unreviewable for lack of a federal question.

to plead claim preclusion as a bar to the assertion of A's claim against him?

On the first of these questions, American courts, backed by the *Restatement (Third) of the Foreign Relations Law of the United States (1987)* (RTFRL), have generally been willing to enforce—and to recognize—foreign country judgments, so long as (1) the foreign judgment satisfies our constitutional standards relating to territorial jurisdiction, adequate notice, and procedural fairness, (2) the judgment was a final one that the foreign country itself would recognize as entitled to recognition and enforcement, and (3) the judgment was not in some way repugnant to the public policy of the forum.[58] The rationale underlying this willingness is similar to that underlying domestic rules of preclusion, combined with a desire to achieve a greater measure of stability and repose in matters involving international relationships. But one of the questions that has divided courts and commentators, and that is presented by the hypothetical, is whether a foreign judgment will be honored if the country that rendered it will not grant reciprocal recognition or enforcement to a judgment of the American forum. The question is a close and difficult one, and resembles in some ways the issues of reciprocity that arise in the area of foreign trade. But the tendency among American courts in recent years has been

58. *See* RTFRL §§ 481–88, and authorities cited in the Reporter's Notes to those sections and in the 2000 Supp. thereto. For the wide acceptance and effect of a uniform act (on the recognition of foreign money judgments) on the practices of the states, see *infra* pp. 161–63.

not to insist on reciprocity as a condition.[59] This trend has some interesting consequences; foremost among them is that the willingness of our courts to give faith and credit to foreign judgments of countries that do not reciprocate (wholly or in part) has given us particular cause to promote—through international understandings—arrangements that will entitle American judgments to greater respect abroad.

If New Jersey does decide to recognize the Fredonia judgment, the next series of questions involves the relevant source of the applicable rules of preclusion. Barring any of the factors noted above, it is unlikely that New Jersey will give *less* credit to the Fredonia judgment than Fredonia would; but should it give more and, if so, how much more? The question raises many of the same issues discussed in the previous sections, but here the answer is unconstrained by any rule of federal law—and interestingly, no clear resolution is proposed by the RTFRL.[60] In the hypothetical, it seems hard to justify giving A, the Fredonian plaintiff, the *benefit* of any New Jersey preclusion rules that go beyond the rules of her own country—for example, by allowing her to invoke issue preclusion in her property damage action against B. After all, such a benefit would be a windfall to A, who chose the original forum for her own convenience and can reasonably

59. *See* Silberman & Lowenfeld, *supra* note 54, at 636.

60. *See* Casad, *supra* note 54, at 53–57 (discussing proposed draft of the RTFRL).

be held to its limitations when it comes to the preclusive effects of its judgments.

But what of B, who was an unwilling defendant in an inconvenient court? May he take advantage of New Jersey's broader definition of a claim to bar a second property damage action in the courts of his home state? The case is a close one, but surely, any unfairness to A of such a result is far from heart-rending (after all, A can still sue B for property damage in Fredonia, if she can get territorial juris-diction over him there).

And what of C? Could he have invoked the benefit of New Jersey's former "entire controversy" doc-trine (assuming that New Jersey's courts believed that the normal prerequisites for its invocation had been met)? As indicated above, pp. 133–34, the arguments against such a result within our federal system are strong, and they appear strong in the international context as well. Unlike B, C did not have to litigate at all in another forum, and thus it does not seem unfair to open him to litigation in New Jersey. (And allowing C to prevail on the basis of claim preclusion would surely not go down well in Fredonia.) Indeed, the only factor weighing sig-nificantly in C's favor is the interest of New Jersey in saving the costs of litigation. And if New Jersey is now the only forum open to A (who had little cause to suspect that its doors would be closed as a result of her prior action against B), that factor may not be enough to tip the scales. But if New Jersey wishes to economize in this way, it is clearly free to do so.

Some of the questions discussed in the preceding paragraphs have been resolved in the Uniform Foreign Money–Judgments Recognition Act, a statute that has been adopted—essentially as drafted by the Commission on Uniform State Laws—in many states, and in somewhat modified form in others, and has influenced the development of the law in almost every jurisdiction.[61] The Act generally provides for the enforcement and recognition of foreign money judgments,[62] subject to the kinds of conditions discussed above. Thus it specifically states that a foreign judgment is not "conclusive" if the rendering court did not have territorial jurisdiction or subject matter jurisdiction,[63] or did not "provide impartial tribunals or procedures compatible with the requirements of due process of law."[64] And of special interest, the Act states that a foreign judg-

61. As of January 2000, 29 states, the District of Columbia, and the Virgin Islands had adopted the UNIFORM FOREIGN MONEY-JUDGMENTS RECOGNITION ACT (UFMJRA), 13 U.L.A. 263 (Supp. 1998), either as drafted or with some variations, and many other states apply the general principles of the Act. *See* Silberman & Lowenfeld, *supra* note 54, at 636 nn. 6, 7.

62. The Act does not deal with the recognition or enforcement of equitable decrees—a subject that is still marked by uncertainty, even at the domestic level, *see supra* p. 120, and also excludes certain categories of actions, notably those involving divorce, custody, and support judgments. In contrast, these topics are dealt with in RTFRL. *See id.* at 593 (Introductory Note).

63. UFMJRA § 4. In contrast, the RTFRL does not make the existence of subject matter jurisdiction a prerequisite of enforcement, although it does provide that the lack of such jurisdiction is a permissible basis for refusal to enforce. *See* RTFRL § 482(2)(a).

64. UFMJRA § 4.

ment may but "need not" be recognized under a variety of circumstances, *e.g.*, if the judgment was obtained by fraud, the forum was "seriously inconvenient," or the foreign court entertained the action despite a forum selection clause in a contract between the parties that provided for exclusive jurisdiction in another forum.[65]

The UFMJRA (please forgive another unpronounceable acronym) has (like other uniform acts) taken a giant step in the direction of desirable uniformity without federal intervention. But not all states have adopted it, some have attached specific "reciprocity" provisions, and not every provision has been given the same interpretation in every state. Moreover, the Act's provision, in Section 3, that the foreign money judgment "is enforceable in the same manner as the judgment of a sister state which is entitled to full faith and credit" somewhat mysteriously does not explicitly refer to "recognition" (though that has been assumed to be included). In any event, Section 3 leaves open the many unresolved questions about the application of the Full Faith and Credit Clause, especially (and importantly, in view of the more limited approach to preclusion in other countries) the appropriateness of giving a judgment more recognition than the rendering court would give. Finally, and perhaps most important, the Act does not directly aid Amer-

65. *See id.* Among other grounds stated in § 4 under which a foreign judgment need not be recognized are: "the [cause of action or claim] on which the judgment is based is repugnant to the public policy of this state," and "the judgment conflicts with another final and conclusive judgment."

ican efforts to achieve a higher level of recognition for this nation's judgments in other countries.

As this discussion suggests, the arguments for federalizing the law in this area (through statute or the development of federal common law) remain strong, as do the advantages to be gained from an international convention that would formalize the reciprocal recognition and enforcement of the judgments of signatory countries and would specify the conditions under which such recognition and enforcement would be required, permitted, or denied.[66] Yet at this writing, efforts to achieve international agreement, after some progress, seem to have foundered, at least temporarily, on several shoals, notably disagreement over the appropriate bases for exercising territorial jurisdiction.[67] In sum, the courts of other countries have been consistently less receptive than have our own courts to territorial jurisdiction founded on such factors as

66. As stated in Silberman & Lowenfeld, *supra* note 54, at 638–39: "[F]oreign judgments are recognized and enforced to a much greater extent in the United States than judgments rendered in the United States are recognized and enforced abroad."

67. The status of negotiations at the Hague, as of the close of 1999, are described by Silberman & Lowenfeld, *supra* note 54. As stated in that article, the proposed convention is to some extent modeled on the Brussels Convention on Jurisdiction and the Enforcement of Judgments in Civil and Commercial Matters, Sept. 27, 1968, 1990 O.J. (C 189) 2 (consolidated), a convention in effect for the 12 countries that were members of the European Union prior to 1995. As indicated in text, and as reported orally to the American Law Institute in May 2000, negotiations looking toward such a convention, to which the United States would be a signatory, have bogged down over several issues, especially those relating to the proper scope of territorial jurisdiction.

the physical presence of an individual in the territory of the forum (so-called "tag" jurisdiction),[68] or to the proper scope of "general" jurisdiction" over corporations and other entities (especially general jurisdiction based not on the place of incorporation but simply on the regularity with which the entity "does business" in the forum).[69] As a result, U.S. participation in the convention might render unenforceable, *both* here and abroad, certain U.S. judgments that satisfy the demands of our own Constitution. Our negotiators have balked at that result.

On a related front, the American Law Institute several years ago launched a project designed to draft federal legislation with an eye to either or both of the following: (1) implementing an international convention if one is agreed to and if the U.S. becomes a signatory, and (2) providing rules for the recognition and enforcement of foreign country judgments if no such convention is agreed to, or in any event with respect to those countries that do

68. The Supreme Court, in Burnham v. Superior Court, 495 U.S. 604 (1990), upheld the constitutionality of this method of exercising territorial jurisdiction over individuals.

69. In an important article published in 1966, and since relied on by commentators and by the Supreme Court, the authors distinguished between "general" jurisdiction (in which the contacts between the defendant and the forum are regarded as sufficient for the assertion of territorial jurisdiction even if those contacts have little or no relationship to the particular claim in suit) and "specific" jurisdiction (in which such a relationship does exist and is critical to the availability of territorial jurisdiction). Arthur T. von Mehren & Donald T. Trautman, *Jurisdiction to Adjudicate: A Suggested Analysis*, 79 Harv. L. Rev. 1121 (1966).

not become signatories to the convention.[70] But because of the interruption of negotiations over the terms of such a convention, the Reporters, in a Memorandum to the ALI Council in late 2000, recommended that the project be refocused on the second aspect of the original project, and the Council agreed.

In sum, much thought is being given, and energy devoted, to the bewildering problems of the recognition and enforcement of foreign judgments. But to date, those efforts have not borne significant fruit.

70. In the spring of 2000, the Reporters for this project, Professors Lowenfeld and Silberman, submitted a report to the Institute describing the project and its relationship to the proposed Hague Convention. *See* AMERICAN LAW INSTITUTE, INTERNATIONAL JURISDICTION AND JUDGMENTS PROJECT, REPORT (2000).

*

TABLE OF CASES

References are to Pages

Aerojet–General Corp. v. Askew, 94
Aetna Life Ins. Co. v. Tremblay, 157
Allen v. McCurry, 136
Amchem Products, Inc. v. Windsor, 89
American Mach. & Metals v. De Bothezat Impeller Co., 63
Arizona v. California, 49, 72
ASARCO Inc. v. Kadish, 143
Ashe v. Swenson, 47

Baker by Thomas v. General Motors Corp., 96, 120, 128
Banco Nacional de Cuba v. Sabbatino, 157
Bartkus v. People of State of Ill., 123
Benson and Ford, Inc. v. Wanda Petroleum Co., 92, 93, 94, 95
Bernhard v. Bank of America Nat. Trust & Savings Ass'n, 107, 108
Blockburger v. United States, 36
Blonder–Tongue Laboratories, Inc. v. University of Illinois Foundation, 109
Board of Public Works v. Columbia College, 131
Burnham v. Superior Court of California, County of Marin, 164

Cambria v. Jeffery, 50
Cauefield v. Fidelity & Cas. Co. of New York, 94
Chicago & Southern Air Lines v. Waterman S.S. Corp., 14
Chicot County Drainage Dist. v. Baxter State Bank, 26
Commissioner v. Sunnen, 53, 55
Cogdell by Cogdell v. Hospital Center at Orange, 104
Cook, Ill., County of, United States v., 27
Costello v. United States, 42
County of (see name of county)

167

Crowell v. Benson, 26

District of Columbia Court of Appeals v. Feldman, 136
Dixon, United States v., 36
Duncan v. United States, 77
Dupasseur v. Rochereau, 148

Epstein v. MCA, Inc., 91
Erie R. Co. v. Tompkins, 147

Fauntleroy v. Lum, 124
Federated Dept. Stores, Inc. v. Moitie, 44, 151
Fidelity Nat. Bank & Trust Co. of Kansas City v. Swope, 143

Gonzales v. Cassidy, 91
Griffin v. State Bd. of Ed., 44

Halpern v. Schwartz, 52
Hansberry v. Lee, 84, 89
Hardy v. Johns–Manville Sales Corp., 93
Haring v. Prosise, 66, 137
Hart v. American Airlines, Inc., 131
Hayburn's Case, 14
Heath v. Alabama, 123
Hilton v. Guyot, 157

Idaho v. Coeur d'Alene Tribe of Idaho, 76

Jeter v. Hewitt, 12

Kalb v. Feuerstein, 27, 143
Kremer v. Chemical Const. Corp., 136, 138

Lee, United States v., 76
Lemonds v. St. Louis County, 136
Lummus Co. v. Commonwealth Oil Refining Co., 30
Lyons v. Westinghouse Electric Corporation, 142
Lytle v. Household Mfg., Inc., 110

Mansfield, C. & L.M. Ry. Co. v. Swan, 29
Marrese v. American Academy of Orthopaedic Surgeons, 140
Martin v. Wilks, 99, 101

Matsushita Elec. Indus. Co., Ltd. v. Epstein, 139
McElmoyle, for Use of Bailey v. Cohen, 120
Mendoza, United States v., 114
Mick v. Mani, 104
Migra v. Warren City School Dist. Bd. of Educ., 131, 136, 138, 139
Montana v. United States, 53, 75
Mortgagelinq Corp. v. Commonwealth Land Title Ins. Co., 131
Moser, United States v., 53
Munsingwear, Inc., United States v., 72

Parklane Hosiery Co., Inc. v. Shore, 109, 151
Parsons Steel, Inc. v. First Alabama Bank, 137
Pelullo, United States v., 47
Pena–Cabanillas v. United States, 47
Phillips Petroleum Co. v. Shutts, 84, 89, 90
Plaut v. Spendthrift Farm, Inc., 14
Provident Tradesmens Bank & Trust Co. v. Patterson, 100

Richards v. Jefferson County, Ala., 96
Riordan v. Ferguson, 11
Rooker v. Fidelity Trust Co., 136

Sawyer v. First City Financial Corp., 36
Semtek Intern. Inc. v. Lockheed Martin Corp., 145, 148
Shaffer v. Heitner, 61
South Central Bell Telephone Co. v. Alabama, 96, 101
Southwest Airlines Co. v. Texas Intern. Airlines, Inc., 94
Spomer v. Littleton, 77
Stauffer Chemical Co., United States v., 53
Stoll v. Gottlieb, 26
Stone & Downer Co., United States v., 60
Supreme Tribe of Ben Hur v. Cauble, 84

Thomas v. Washington Gas Light Co., 129
Tice v. American Airlines, Inc., 93
Treinies v. Sunshine Mining Co., 132
Tyus v. Schoemehl, 94, 96

United States v. _____ (see opposing party)
United States Bancorp Mortg. Co. v. Bonner Mall Partnership, 72
United States Fidelity & Guar. Co., United States v., 26, 143
University of Tennessee v. Elliott, 68

Vanderveer v. Erie Malleable Iron Co., 142

Watkins v. Conway, 121
White v. Adler, 44
Williams v. Taylor, 144

Yarborough v. Yarborough, 122
York v. Texas, 123

INDEX

References are to pages

ACRONYMS DEFINED
"NMIP," "NMDIP," "NMOIP," 106
"RSJ," 7n
"RTFRL," 158
"UFMJRA," 161n

"ACTUALLY LITIGATED"
As prerequisite to issue preclusion, 48–50

ADMINISTRATIVE PROCEEDINGS
Preclusive effect of adjudications in subsequent civil proceedings, 67–68, 121–22n

ADVERSARINESS
As prerequisite to preclusive effect, 70–71

ALTERNATIVE GROUNDS OF DECISION
Availability of issue preclusion with respect to, 51–53

AGREEMENT
Effects of, 77–78, 139–40

APPEAL
Availability of, as prerequisite to issue preclusion, 49–53, 56–57n
Mootness while appeal is pending, effects of, 72–73

ARBITRATION
Preclusive effects of award in subsequent civil proceedings, 67–68, 121–22n, 155–56n

171

BAR
See also Claim Preclusion
Definition, 10
General rule, 32, 39–41
Exceptions, 41–44

CAUSE OF ACTION
See Claim

CLAIM
Definition, 34–39
Merger and bar, 10

CLAIM PRECLUSION
General rule, 32–34
Exceptions, 41–45
Non-parties, application to, 74–105
Represented persons, application to, 81–97

CLASS ACTIONS
Absent class members, application of preclusion doctrine to, 83–92
Adequacy of representation, relevance to availability of collateral attack, 90–92

COLLATERAL ESTOPPEL
See also Issue Preclusion
Definition, 11

COMPARATIVE PRECLUSION LAW
Preclusion rules of other countries compared to rules in the United States, 15–16, 154–55n

CONTROL OF LITIGATION
Effect of, on availability of preclusion, 75–77

COUNTERCLAIMS
Compulsory counterclaim statutes and rules, effects of, 39, 151
Consequences of failure to interpose in absence of controlling statute or rule, 39

COURTS
See also Federal courts, State courts
Jurisdiction
Subject matter, 25–29
Territorial, 24–25

CRIMINAL JUDGMENTS
Acquittals, effects of in subsequent civil proceedings, 65
Convictions, effects of in subsequent civil proceedings, 64–65
Guilty pleas and pleas of nolo contendere: effects of in subsequent civil proceedings, 66–67

DAMAGES
Effect of judgment for plaintiff on subsequent action for increased damages, 37

DECLARATORY JUDGMENTS
Preclusive effects of, 62–64

DEFAULT JUDGMENTS
Preclusive effects of, 48–49n, 91–92

DIRECT ESTOPPEL
See also Issue preclusion
Definition, 11

DISMISSAL
Preclusive effects of, 39–44

DOUBLE JEOPARDY
Rules of, compared to rules of preclusion in civil actions, 7, 29–30n, 36n, 47n, 123n

ELECTION OF REMEDIES
Distinguished from preclusion, 8–9

ENFORCEMENT OF JUDGMENTS
Distinguished from recognition of judgments, 5–6, 120

"ENTIRE CONTROVERSY" DOCTRINE
Definition and application, 103–05, 131n, 160

"ESSENTIAL TO THE JUDGMENT"
Requirement of, as prerequisite of application of issue preclusion to prior determination, 50–53

ESTOPPEL
See also Issue Preclusion
By verdict, 10
Direct and collateral, 11

FAMILY LAW
See also Status
Custody and support, 62, 122n, 155–56n
Marriage, divorce, and separation, 62

FEDERAL COURTS
See also Courts, State courts
Preclusive effects of judgments
In other federal courts, 151–53
In state courts, 144–51

FEDERAL RULES OF CIVIL PROCEDURE
Rule 8(c), 71
Rule 12(g), (h), 24
Rule 13(a), 39,151
Rule 18, 33
Rule 23, 87–88
Rule 41, 42–43n, 149
Rule 60(b), 6–7, 25

FIDUCIARY
As representative of non-party, 81–83

FINALITY
As prerequisite to preclusive effect, 29–32

FOREIGN COUNTRY JUDGMENTS
International agreements, 155–56, 163–64
Preclusive effects of, in courts of the United States, 153–65

FULL FAITH AND CREDIT
Constitutional and statutory provisions relating to judgments
Requirements of, as applied to judgments of state courts, 121–44
Requirements of, as applied to judgments of federal courts, 144–51

HABEAS CORPUS
Generally, 7

INTERJURISDICTIONAL PRECLUSION
See also Federal courts, State courts, Foreign country judgments
Generally, 119–65

INTERNATIONAL AGREEMENTS
See Foreign country judgments

ISSUE PRECLUSION
General rule, 46–56
Exceptions, 56–60
Non-parties, application to, 74–103, 105–16
Represented persons, application to, 81–97

JOINDER
Failure to intervene as a party, consequences of, 97–102, 109–10
Failure to join a person as a party, consequences of, 42, 103–05,
    131n, 160

JUDGMENTS
As "operative fact," 116–18
Consent, 48–49n, 139–40
Criminal, 64–67
Declaratory, 62–64
Default, 48–49n
"On the merits," 39–44, 148–50
Preclusive effects of
    In the same jurisdiction, 22–118
    In other jurisdictions, 119–65
    With respect to parties, 22–73
    With respect to non-parties, 74–118
Prerequisites to recognition, 23–32

JURISDICTION
As prerequisite to validity of judgment
    Subject matter jurisdiction, 25–29
    Territorial jurisdiction, 24–25
Dismissal for lack of, 42
In rem and quasi-in-rem, 60–62

LAW OF THE CASE
Distinguished from preclusion, 8

MERGER
    See also Claim Preclusion
Definition, 10
General rule, 32–41
    Exceptions, 44–45

MOOTNESS
On appeal, effect of, 72–73

MUTUALITY
Definition, 102–03
Requirement of, as basis for preclusion
    Arguments for and against, 103–18
    Developments in the law relating to, 103–18

NMIP, NMDIP, NMOIP
See Acronyms defined

NON–JUDICIAL PROCEEDINGS
Generally, 67–68, 121–22n

NON–PARTIES
See also Mutuality

Persons treated as if they were parties, 75–97

Preclusive effects of a judgment with respect to non-parties to
    that judgment
  "Benefits" of a prior judgment
    Claim preclusion, 103–05
    Issue preclusion, 105–18
  "Burdens" of a prior judgment, 75–102

NOTICE
As prerequisite to preclusive effect of judgment, 24–25

"ON THE MERITS"
As used in the Federal Rules of Civil Procedure, 149–50

Avoidance of term in Restatement of Judgments, reasons for,
    39–41

PARTIES
See also Adversariness, Non-parties

Definition for purposes of the rules of preclusion, 68–71

PRECLUSION
See also Claim preclusion, Issue preclusion

Other doctrines distinguished, 5–9

Rationale for rules of, 11–21

PRIVITY
See also Parties, Non-parties

Avoidance of term in Restatement of Judgments, 81n

PROCEDURAL ISSUES
Generally, 71–73

Failure to assert preclusive effect, consequences of, 71–72

Mootness on appeal, 72–73

REAL PARTY IN INTEREST
Generally, 69–70

RELIEF FROM JUDGMENTS
Bases for, 25, 37n, 73

Distinguished from questions of recognition, 6–7

REPRESENTATION
See also Virtual representation
As basis for preclusion, 81–97

RES JUDICATA
See also Claim preclusion, Issue preclusion
Definition, 9–11

RESTATEMENT OF JUDGMENTS
Generally, 1–3
Influence on law of preclusion, 1

ROOKER–FELDMAN DOCTRINE
Definition, 136n
Preclusion distinguished, 136n

RSJ
See Acronyms defined

RTFRL
See Acronyms defined

SETTLEMENTS
Preclusive effects of, 40, 48–49n, 139

STATE COURTS
See also Courts, Federal courts
Preclusive effects of judgments
In courts of other states, 121–35
In federal courts, 135–44

STATUS
Judgments adjudicating, preclusive effects of, 62

STATUTE OF LIMITATIONS
Preclusive effects of dismissal based on, 41, 126–27

TRANSACTION
As basis for determining scope of a "claim," 34–39

TRUSTEE
See Fiduciary

UFMJRA
See Acronyms defined

UNIFORM FOREIGN MONEY–JUDGMENTS RECOGNITION ACT
Generally, 161–63

VALIDITY OF JUDGMENT
As prerequisite to preclusive effect, 23–29

VENUE
Dismissal for lack of, 42

"VIRTUAL" REPRESENTATION
    See also Representation, Non-parties
As basis for preclusion of non-party, 92–97

†